2·99

THE GRAEME PULLEN GUIDE TO
Freshwater Fishing Baits

The Oxford Illustrated Press

The Oxford Illustrated Press

© 1988, Graeme Pullen

Reprinted 1991.

ISBN 0 946609 73 X

Published by:
The Oxford Illustrated Press Limited, Haynes Publishing Group, Sparkford, Nr Yeovil, Somerset BA22 7JJ, England.

Haynes Publications Inc., 861 Lawrence Drive, Newbury Park, California 91320, USA.

Printed in England by:
J.H. Haynes & Co Limited, Sparkford, Nr. Yeovil, Somerset.

British Library Cataloguing in Publication Data
Pullen, Graeme
   Freshwater fishing baits.
   1. Freshwater angling. Baits
   I. Title
   799.1'1
   ISBN 0-946609-73-X

Library of Congress Catalog Card Number
88-80361

Dedication

To someone who will never be born.
The angler who knows it all!

Acknowledgements

This book has been researched, written, illustrated, typed (one-fingered!) and compiled all on my lonesome, in between customers in one of my retail shops. Although I had progressed to the concept of fishing books following the success at my first attempt at book writing: *Big Game Fishing: The Great Adventure* I did not realise just how quickly I could work if the research material was available. But to do that research I needed the help of several people. Firstly, I would like to thank Hilary for her attempts to stop me writing all hours in order to do her household jobs (they still aren't done!) and Clive Dietrich and Malcolm Winkworth who let me keep them from their tea one June evening when they really had better things to do.

Thanks are also due to the Somerset Bait Co who let me loose in the flyhouses and maggot pits to research my material about maggot production. To their amusement I came away with flies up my nose, in my ears, down my neck, and up my trouser legs and inside my car. Never, ever, will I forget that Sunday morning that is still giving me nightmares. Well, if you were confronted in a dark warehouse with $3^1/2$ tons of dead baby chickens, 500 gallons of maggots and four million flies (a conservative estimate) wouldn't you have nightmares?

Lastly thanks go to managers Dave Barraball and Nigel Newport of Western Fuels Tackle shop in my home town of Fleet, for letting me loose in their stockroom. Apart from the live wasp cake it was nowhere near the league of that maggot farm, and was a pleasure to work in.

I suppose too, that I had better acknowledge the customers I have lost through not answering their queries on furniture designs, only grunting as I wanted to finish my typing. Please come back . . . I need the money!

Contents

Introduction

When I looked at what was available to the freshwater fisherman in the way of illustrated information on baits, I found nothing. At first I thought I would write a magazine article on the subject but then I thought about the restrictions imposed on good illustrations and changed my mind: I would do better to write a book.

I am not an editor, a sub-editor or a layout designer, I am an angler, and I know what the anglers want because I fish with them. I have always been an angler first, photographer second, and writer third, so it was a major decision to change from writing 800 words for a newspaper, to creating 30,000 words for a book. Yet I was 'gung-ho' on this new bait book: my enthusiasm was such that I researched like a demented reporter, and shot film like a fashion photographer.

Anglers will always experiment with, and search for, new baits, different colourings and more fragrant flavourings. Between these pages I have tried to cram as much *basic* information as I can. The list of baits that fish have been caught on is endless. What I have tried to do is mention, and where possible illustrate, such baits as I have had fish on myself. For those of you who are taking a PhD in the thermo-molecular structure of the three dimensional boilie, read no further. You will not read of amino acid analysis breakdowns in this book. Also within this text I thought the two most popular baits of the present day surely deserved a little more explanation; a bit more in-depth research. You all know where a maggot and a boilie comes from? Yes, the local tackle shop. But they don't grow there you know and they have a beginning far removed from the fridge or groundbait counter. So in the chapters 'The Maggot Farm' and 'The Boilie Boom', I thought you would like to know how, where and why they started. It won't catch you more fish, but there might be a few facts, and certainly a few illustrations to make it more interesting. I have also taken a light hearted look at weird baits of the past and a few of the present in the chapter 'Baits of Yesteryear'.

I have always been told that if I was going to do something, to do it properly. I wish I could say I applied this philosophy to my fishing, but you'll be overjoyed to learn I am writing this introduction at Lodge Pond in Surrey, with dodgy optonics that register one beep every three feet of line! So far in between fishing and writing I have cracked off one carp, and missed two bream bites! Hopefully you will find the book informative, interesting and in parts entertaining. I really must get these optonics seen to, but you'll be pleased to know I just netted a 3-lb bream . . . and on trout pellet paste as well!

The Boilie Boom

Those anglers not wishing to continue with maggots in the belief that a bigger bait catches a bigger fish, will now be able to look towards 'instant' hookbaits that need no previous preparation. These are called boilies, and they are currently available in most tackle shops, supplied by a number of different manufacturers. These boilies are full of protein, are nutritional, and come in a variety of flavours and colours; so that is where the next step in advanced professional baits will lead to.

But first let's look back at the carp angling scene, which is where the boilies originated. It was in the 50s that carp fishing received the boost in publicity it needed, when 'Clarissa', the famous 44-lb record Redmire carp was caught by the late Dick Walker. I know records are always there to be beaten, but I reckon a lot of anglers will agree with me that this must surely go down as the most stunning carp record of all time. Certainly, it has left many current-day carp over 40 lb in the 'just another big carp' category as far as publicity goes.

In those early days the best baits were flake, crust and potatoes—the latter par-boiled with a crust pad on the base to take the impact of casting. From there anglers moved into a 'meat' phase, with sausage meat and pastes (and also cheeses) replacing plain breadflake. The use of cheese and meat undoubtedly made anglers aware of the 'smell' factor of carp baits, and so they began to experiment with the more aromatic dog and cat foods. Pastes were mixed up and carp catch rates soared. Additives like Bisto, curry powder, aniseed and different flavoured stock cubes enhanced baits still further, until along came a man called Fred Wilton.

Fred's theory was that a carp actually knew what baits were nutritionally good for it, and hence the birth of HNV baits (High Nutritional Value). Could a carp actually swim round the lake and decide which were the best baits to eat? Many anglers disagreed vigorously with Fred's belief, but how difficult it is to argue when a theory becomes a practical success. Whether or not carp have that much intelligence is still a matter for conjecture, but it is fact that the HNV baits put carp on the bank in a big way. Fred's baits had bases derived from milk proteins, (lactalbumin, casein and caseinates) for the protein, soya flour for the fat content, and equivite for mineral and vitamins. I used equivite in its neat stages myself and published an article in one of the first *Coarse Fisherman* issues extolling its virtues.

Trout Pellets

Fred's development into this field pushed anglers towards higher protein baits, based on trout pellets—a very high protein feed used in trout farms—where the food was introduced in either pellet or powder form, depending on the different year classes of the fish being fed. Subsequent to this I found out that even higher protein was obtainable from salmon farms, who used maximum high protein in powder granule form for the salmon fry in order to bring them on quickly to a secure growth stage. Amazingly TP (trout pellet) pastes have stood the test of time, and I still smile when some youngster tells me that TP is no good on such-and-such a lake, that it finished ten years ago and that now you need the latest triple-Y protein mix with overhead cams or whatever. The fortunate thing is that nobody has ever told the fish that TP has finished. Fish aren't dictated to by fashion or trends even if anglers are. If a bait tastes good they eat it, providing the fear factor in picking it up is minimal. With everybody else using everything *but* TP paste, I fish with the knowledge that the fear factor is minimal and still put carp and tench on the bank using it. By adding different flavour concentrates to the mix, it is easy to go a couple of years at waters altering only the flavouring, yet retaining TP as the basic paste mix. Even as I write this I have taken (on a June evening in 1987) nine tench from an alleged 'dead' water in Surrey frequented by the local carp youngsters. Every fish fell to TP with strawberry flavouring!

Moving on from this stage in the late 70s to the early 80s, carp anglers progressed to making their own different protein mixes, using certain basic ingredients with as many different colourings and flavourings as they could. At the same time, something else became quickly apparent: anglers were showing a preference for size and quantity of baits they were putting in the water.

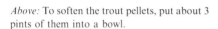

Above: To soften the trout pellets, put about 3 pints of them into a bowl.

Below: Pour in enough boiling water to cover, and leave for 25 seconds.

Above right: Put a lid or plate over the bowl and strain off the water.

Right: Add about a capful of flavouring.

Bottom right: Mash the pellets into a paste. When cool, knead into balls of softer paste. Freeze some if all aren't needed straightaway.

While many anglers believed you needed big baits for the most smell in the water, there were other anglers who fished the same baits, but used a smaller size and introduced them into the water in much greater quantities. This was known as particle saturation and was generally applied by anglers using seed baits on new waters. I even found myself that there was, or seemed to be, an optimum size bait that got the carp feeding avidly. Although the task of rolling out three hundred thumbnail size balls of TP paste is laborious, once I introduced them into my swim, I can honestly say that I rarely fished a five-hour evening session, when I didn't hook, land or lose a double-figure carp. I also found that I was hacking out tench, roach and bream on these smaller paste sizes as well. This was purely my own experience of course, but working on the premise that there is nothing new in angling, there must have been other anglers doing the same.

Boilies

Once these home-made baits and their success had become established it was of course but a short while before someone tried to make them in quantity, and on a commercial basis. Today you can walk into your local tackle shop and pick up as many boilies as you need, in whatever colour or flavour you choose, and in a choice of three different forms—frozen, ready-to-use or powder. With frozen boilies you are liable to waste some because once defrosted they have to be either used or thrown away. The ready-to-use boilies are popular but have a restricted 'shelf life' and in the early days some of the formulas proved to be not quite right and several tackle dealers found their stock almost sprouting legs and walking off! For these reasons and for reasons of economy and flexibility, the powders have proved most successful. From the powder ingredients and commercially available flavourings (which are cheaper than either of the other ready-made boilies), any angler can not only make his own mix and quantity but can choose whether to make them for immediate use or to freeze all or some of them. I decided to visit one of the market leaders in boilies and boilie mixes to give you an insight into their operations.

Started by Clive Dietrich and Malcolm Winkworth, they began their trail to success in 1984, although both had dabbled in bait mixing for many years before this. Clive in fact started out making Readymix, the first commercially available HP carp bait for anglers. Both men are anglers themselves which makes their knowledge of what the carp requires, great indeed. Their catch statistics make me feel quite envious, with Malcolm having taken six 30-lb-plus fish and sixty or seventy 20s, while Clive has taken over twenty 30-lb-plus fish to 44 lb, and around 150 20s. Amazing figures—but then they are both dedicated big carp specialists and for this reason I find it no surprise that both anglers love to use boilie baits.

Clive and Malcolm operated from Fetcham in Surrey, and one evening I shut up business early to drive over to see them. They told me that they started along with many other anglers mixing their eggs and flavourings, until in 1984 they cracked the notoriously hard fishing of the Colne Valley waters. From this success they decided to go into the bait business, and started their first production from a small garage. Although they started with the production of powders for anglers to mix themselves, they soon added ready-made boilies to their range. At that time many anglers were still making their own boilies from fresh ingredients, so to win them over and to stop them 'doing their own thing', they extended the choice of boilies to twelve different kinds. Both a competitive price and instant availability of a wide variety of colours and flavours were factors used to encourage anglers to use the shop variety. Their marketing certainly worked for me, for to be honest, with such a range now available I don't bother to mix my own any more. It really isn't worth all that hassle in the kitchen, the time and the mess, when for a few pounds you get the same thing, and can go fishing straight away.

At the peak of their business they could offer no less than 48 products which are available in about 500 tackle shops. The frozen boilie sales are very strong but it is the 'shelf-life' boilie that is the new thing. They have 30 varieties scheduled in the range and sell at the peak start-of-the-season period . . . wait . . . a staggering ten tons of boilies a week. While I was at the factory I witnessed a change of shift workers as they go right through the night to keep up with demand. While the visit to the maggot farm was a severe strain on my nostrils and stomach muscles, I felt more like I had crashed into the cosmetic counter at Boots when I walked into their factory. Perfumed scents and bright coloured boilies were everywhere, giving me the urge to scoop up all the loose ones on the floor and rush out to catapult them in to Yateley North Pit! The best sellers are the Tutti Frutti, Salmon Supreme and Honey Yucatan flavours.

Now of course you don't just have to buy a ready flavoured bait. You can buy the new multi-coloured neutral boilie then atomise your own spray flavour on to it. That gives you a mammoth selection of choice, and more than you are ever going to need in one season. There are over 60 different flavours available in atomiser sprays alone, indeed I am told that some anglers are beginning to spray them on maggots!

For the angler still wishing to mix his own boilies, and thereby perhaps make a larger size bait, he can buy the 50/50 pack of protein mix. This is a terrific seller and consists of 50% protein and 50% minerals, roughage and carbohydrates, and comes in a 5-lb pack. Mixed properly you should get a couple of thousand small boilies from it. Even if you make only a thousand larger ones they still only work out roughly at 1p each. Clive explained that Europe is the most exciting market, especially Germany where anglers are just getting into the boilie boom. They exported some 500 bags a week to Europe, making up to a thousand bags a week with the British portion of the market.

My trip through the factory started with an amazing machine. It looked like a stainless steel monster from Star Wars, but was in fact an American egg cracking machine, which can crack an astounding 10,000 eggs an hour! I should hate to get my finger caught in that! They still use eggs for their mixes, and obviously bulk buy eggs from a commercial source. The eggs are cracked open to mix their liquid with the relevant powder, the volume of eggs being up to 1,000 kilos in a week. Two huge commercial food mixing machines stood churning by the side, and an employee shovelled scoops of pink colouring into the massive bowls. They mix up 48 lb of powder into a paste at one time, and when the mix is at the required consistency with flavourings and colourings added, the mix is transferred to an automatic boilie machine. This Clive would not let me photograph, as for reasons obvious to all, a machine designed specifically for stamping out some 2,000 boilies a minute into 16mm sizes, is something he did not wish his competitors to learn about. Once they come out of the "boilie basher" they are scooped into a vast boiler and cooked for between three and four minutes. Once cooled, they are bagged and blast-frozen down to await delivery to the different tackle shops. For the new shelf-life variety the procedure is exactly the same, but they are only blanched, not boiled, before being baked in trays to form the commercial shelf-life boilie. Malcolm's advice for keeping the shelf-life boilies is to store them in a dry atmosphere and most important to keep them out of direct sunlight.

The general-purpose boilie is for use as a bottom-fished bait, but anglers also need to have a floating variety for special conditions, or when fish are moving near the surface. The floaters receive the same treatment but are baked for twice as long as the shelf-life ones to make sure they float.

The American market has yet to open up, but having been there carp fishing myself I can see that very shortly the carp anglers of North and South Carolina will catch on to the boilie boom. While I was there I fished with Bruce Vaughan of Ryobi Masterline Tackle, and in two days on a North Carolina lake we took some 250 lb of carp. Our host knocked spots off us with what resembled a bolt rig with a rice pack on puffed wheat bait, and our HPs seemed slow. Their tactics looked crude compared to our own, and the only way I picked up four doubles was to take them off the surface on a single grain of Sugar Puff fished on a flyrod! Not the most conventional method, but then I always have had a reputation for diversity! Other countries that boilies have found a good following in are Holland and Belgium. They take some 4 tons a week in to Europe and these represents some 30 per cent of the business.

Every colouring and flavouring is perfectly safe for human

consumption, and when I talked with Bob Burchett, an avid carp angler, he told me he often sampled the new flavoured boilies when they came in the shop to see what they were like. Now that's what I call dedication! The flavourings are purchased in 25-kilo drums, then mechanically poured into the 50-ml bottles available in the tackle shops.

Popular among barbel fishermen are the recently introduced 'mini boilies'. Only some 4mm in diameter, a couple of cartons give you a day's supply that will drive the fish crazy. So far I have only hammered the tench on these, but I feel sure they will become an important bait in the particle saturation method of fishing.

When the trout pellet boom or HP bait 'blew out' (as I mentioned earlier it hasn't blown for me yet), then seed baits took over. However the seed baits won't hold fish for as long as boilies. Like any new bait that is successful, the boilie had some initial criticism. A ban was even imposed in the north because they thought boilies would break down and ferment on the bottom, but this has never been proven. Now they are used to such an extent, and are so high in HNV and HP values, that the carp actually put on weight and depend on boilies as an integral part of their diet on hard-fished waters. Two bags of boilies should be sufficient for a weekend session, with around 250-300 baits for every 24 hours, though naturally it depends how many bites you are getting and how many are being eaten.

Remember that the boilie boom is still relatively new to most anglers, and although brought about by the advancements of the carp anglers, the boilie you can buy today will also put many other species on the bank. The boiled ham flavour is especially good for barbel, while Salmon Supreme plays havoc with a shoal of tench, and the flavourings when added to your groundbait are excellent for pulling the roach off the angler in the next peg during a match or pleasure session.

Boilies are here to stay in a big way, and are one of the new successful alternatives available to the modern angler who has to keep pace with tactics and changes. While I have no immediate desire to return to the maggot farm, my visit to the factory had made a pleasant evening during which I learnt quite a bit. It just goes to show just how much more goes into the making of a professionally supplied bait.

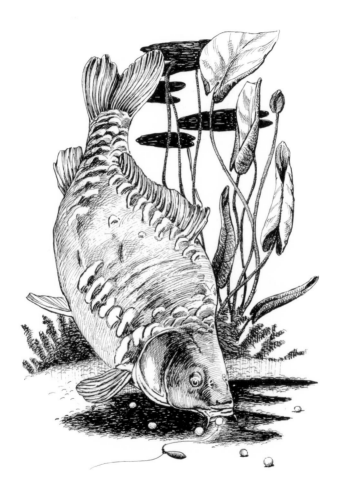

Facing page: Correctly mixed, soft, hand-rolled paste baits like trout pellets, are still very successful for a wide variety of species, especially carp.

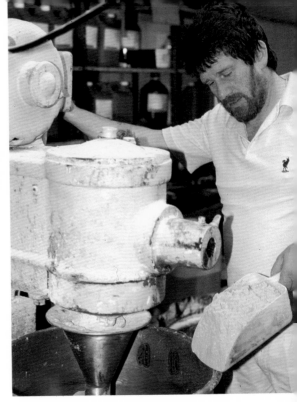

First in the process of boilie making is the addition of the powders to give them colouring and flavour.

Commercial food processors mix the paste which is then put into a moulding machine.

Facing page: In the river, chub as well as barbel will take boilies if they are introduced into the swim regularly. Here is a fine pair of chub landed on wild cherry flavoured boilies.

Once stamped into shape, the boilies are baked in the oven.

The end product: hundreds of multi-coloured 50/50 boilies.

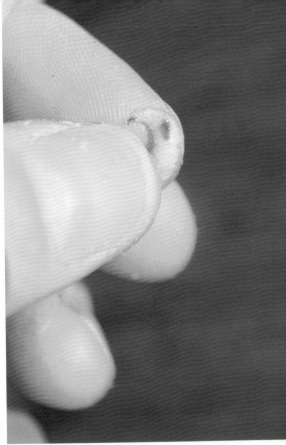

Above left: How a maggot changes to a caster 1. The white maggot slows its movements. 2. When it stops it gets shorter. 3. It gets darker by the day. 4. The best casters are a light golden brown. 5. Useless for fishing, this one has stretched into a skin.

Above right: This black 'feed spot' shows the maggot is fresh.

Left: Plain white maggots—popular with everyone.

Facing page

Top left: Maggots dyed yellow for river fishermen.

Top right: Maggots which have become red because of the dye sprinkled on their food at the maggot farm.

Bottom left: One of the latest match baits — red casters from red maggots.

Bottom right: Maggots, small though they are, can catch big fish—like this 17lb-plus carp.

Nigel Newport unhooks
bream taken on bron
maggots (inset).

Part of a 300-lb-plus haul taken from the River Inny, Ireland in under 6 hours, on casters (inset).

Down on the Maggot Farm!

As with other types of fishing, whether sea, coarse or game fishing, there is one bait that is most popular, that popularity generally being due to convenience of collection. In that connection I would say that every freshwater angler must have at some time or other used maggots on the hook and I would assume with the versatility of this tiny bait, that they will have caught fish on it. A live, wriggling offering introduced in some quantity to a swim can catch virtually any sized fish from the first year fry sought after by the match fisherman with his pole, right up to a double-figure carp that can engulf a bunch of twenty maggots impaled on a size-2 Partridge carp hook. Many years ago the dedicated freshwater angler would hang a chicken liver in a tree at the bottom of a garden and let nature do the rest. From this he would get enough maggots — if carefully managed — to last for a short session. Today, the emphasis is more on quantity than quality, and the average angler wants enough maggots to hold a large shoal of fish in a confined area. Probably the average use per angler would be about two pints for a session, which is still a lot of maggots — and he needs to acquire them quickly, with the minimum amount of fuss.

Almost every tackle shop serving the freshwater angling community will be selling maggots, mainly to draw fishermen in through the door. Many anglers just can't walk past that float, hook or reel counter without buying something that they probably don't need anyway! These are the people that keep the tackle shops in business. The shops earn very little on the maggots, as they must be competitively priced in order to bring the anglers in, and nursing the maggots is labour intensive. At my local tackle shop in Fleet, the manager, Nigel Newport, in early season is daily at work running off casters, riddling off dead skins and generally ensuring the customer gets a value-for-money product. It's not a job many of us would like to do ourselves, although we always moan about the extravagant price for this 'white gold'.

Facing page: Carp were the main species to make nut baits popular. Inset: maples, tic peas and tiger nuts—note the cooked tiger nuts are twice the size of the uncooked ones.

Freshwater Fishing Baits

In compiling this bait book, I decided I should take you behind the scenes, to let you see not only how a commercial maggot farm works, but why the price of a pint of maggots is what it is today. After many phone calls I managed to establish contact with Terry Hiscocks, whose company supplies many tackle shops with bait. I discussed my idea of writing about exactly how things ran in a big maggot farm and so a meeting was set up for me at the Somerset Bait Co., which is run by Terry and his partner Charlie Barnes. I took directions to reach the farm from Terry, but couldn't place it exactly as it was located out in the Somerset country. 'Just get to the top of the hill' said Terry, 'and don't worry about looking for it, you'll smell it first!' Little was I to know just how right he was.

After a 2^1/$_2$ hour drive from Fleet I came to the hill, saw what looked like a warehouse with two skips outside and stepped out to take a better look. That was mistake number one: the stench hit me as soon as I opened the car door. Mistake number two was even to consider taking on the job of going to the farm. You are lucky, I can't put the smell down on paper! I've minced mackerel for sharking trips. I've mashed up rotten pollock for tope, but I promise you that nothing, simply nothing can be compared to the smell exuding from the doorway of that building!

At the farm there appeared to be nobody about so I edged inside the darkened warehouse door, where I suddenly realised that my new cuban leather boots were an inch thick in offal and mush. In front of me was about three tons of rotting 'something' all in plastic bags, split at the sides. Through the half light I saw some figures and shouted out to them. Manager Rodney Dunford came to meet me, Terry had forewarned him about my trip, and he was ready to give me the full guided tour. Terry was just twenty, and had worked on the farm for some four years, which in these conditions made him something of an old hand. It was June, a week after the season had opened and they were going flat out trying to keep pace with half the nation's demand for early-season maggots.

'I'll show you round' said Rodney, 'but it's a pity you haven't got wellies, it gets a bit gunky at times.' I looked at my boots which already had three bluebottles trying to lay eggs on the top of the slimy

26

gunk covering them. Still, it had to be done so we left for a narrow stairway leading upstairs, to what many would consider their worst nightmare come true: the fly rooms. Rodney disappeared from view in the blackness and I stood in the doorway waiting for the lights to come on. Sensing I had stopped he came back down.

'Can't put any lights on' he said, 'we have to keep everything as dark as possible. Don't panic is the answer, just walk slowly along behind me and wait for your eyes to adjust.'

The smell as I walked upstairs was unreal. You could have cut it into chunks and posted it back home.

What the hell is this room?' I asked, feeling like a Victorian nun in a sailor's pub.

'This is the store room where we keep the fly feed' he said. 'They have to eat something so we feed them up on raw cane sugar. This stuff is sweating a bit though, that's why it smells.'

I hastily followed through into a long corridor, completely blackened and looking like the inside of Alcatraz, with small view screens into rooms 25 feet long and 10 feet wide. I confess to feeling panicky as the overpowering smell and sense of the unknown closed in on me. I peered through a viewing screen to see something like a scene from an Alfred Hitchcock movie. I had expected to see flies obviously; they didn't call them the fly rooms for nothing, but here there were a quarter of a million bluebottles crawling everywhere.

'I'll just take a shot through the viewing window' I said, secretly knowing it was unlikely to come out.

'No, it won't come out' said Rodney, 'you have to get in there with them to get a good shot.' The things I do for anglers!

'Don't panic when the first few flies land on you, you'll soon get used to it. It's important not to move fast, or make any sudden movements that makes them come off the walls.'

Come off the walls! As the flies landed on my face, arms, eyes, nose, etc, it would be about a minute before I was climbing up them!

Once in the room we squatted down, and amazingly I was still alive!

'Why is that window blackened out Rodney?'

'If we rushed in here, the whole quarter of a million flies would take to the wing and rush for the light. They would crush themselves against the glass, so we don't want that. This is the reason we have no electric. If you struck a match they would all rush for it.'

On the floor were several black plastic sheets. On these were placed rotting pouting, obtained from Brixham docks, on which the flies would 'blow', or lay their eggs, The pouting are filleted to expose the flesh, and flies 'blow' better on fish than they would on say, chicken. The walls were black with bluebottles, but none were on the ceiling, which was clear except for droplets of water. I started taking pictures, but the heat from the flies' bodies was so great that both my lenses steamed up. I started to sweat, and realised the droplets on the ceiling were caused by the flies' body heat pushing up the humidity. The flies have to drink water, and get through a fantastic TWO GALLONS of water every day! Hanging from one end of the room to the other were what looked like washing lines. They were in fact folded sheets of newspapers on which the flies could clean themselves, as well as giving them additional landing space.

Along the edge of each wall was a long shelf. On the left-hand side was placed thousands of casters. The average bluebottle will only live for ten to twelve days before dying so it is important to keep a rotation basis of new stock, which are required to hatch out every eight days. The judgement of when the casters are going to hatch into new stock is quite critical. On the other shelf was some brown muck. This was the raw cane sugar which the flies eat. You know how small a bluebottle is? Well, this one flyhouse eats its way through 8 lb of raw sugar in one day alone . . . and Somerset Bait Co. have thirteen fly houses! They all have to be heated during the winter to keep that humidity level up.

The average fly will lay 20 to 40 eggs, taking only one day to lay their eggs on the rotten fish. This is when everything moves on to the next phase.

After seeing all the fly rooms and generally getting the 'heeby-jeebies' from those blackened corridors, Rodney said, 'If you've got all your pictures, I'll take you down to the pits.'

Down to where?

Never mind, it was too late now.

Maggots

Once the flies have laid their eggs on the pouting the sheets are taken downstairs to where the entire warehouse floor has been sectioned off into rows of 15 ft by 10 ft pits with walls about 2 feet high. The fish and eggs are put into the pits with the black plastic sheeting over the top of them to keep the temperature and humidity constant. They hatch overnight and next morning, after they are shaken off the plastic, the pits are covered with minced rotten chicken. On an average day's 'blow' or egg-lay, the production at this stage will be between 3 and 400 gallons of maggots. This is a massive overstocking per pit, so the stock is divided into 12 or 15 pits. At that initial stage with 400 gallons of maggots in one pit, the stench of ammonia is overpowering. I actually had to stand near a 40-gallon drum of sawdust to recover, the smell of minced wood, being better than that of minced chicken and maggots!

They start that initial feed with at least one wheelbarrow of minced baby chickens per pit, and then top up with chicken as they devour it, for some five days. When the maggots are as fully grown as possible the men step in the pits with wellies, and starting from the centre, fork the chicken carcasses and maggots to heaps at either side. Then the bottom of the pit is scattered with sawdust to soak everything up, including the mush. Five old breadbaskets are stacked in metal racking down the centre of the pits and the chicken carcasses and maggots forked into these. The maggots fall through the bottom of these baskets, leaving just the carcasses in the trays. These trays are taken outside and dumped in a skip. From here, once the skip is full, it is taken away to be buried. The skips I can assure you, are not a sight for the weak of stomach or delicate of nose. There should now be roughly thirty gallons of top grade maggots in each pit, from where they are taken to a commercial riddling machine for final separation from what's left of the chicken carcasses. They are then refrigerated at about two gallons to a small tray, from where they find their way into the tackle shops. This whole process takes little more than a week, and produces what the tackle dealers call 'young' maggots. It gives them the maximum length of time to sell them to anglers as good maggots, before they start to change to casters. Provided they are stored in a proper commercial fridge the tackle

Maggots

shops should be able to hold them for one to two weeks before they turn to casters.

In the Somerset Bait Company's refrigerator they hold about 300 gallons at a fraction over freezing temperature, so the body of the maggot slows right down until it hardly moves, but without the risk of frost killing it. The massive pile of bags containing the feed comes from Ross and Buxted chicken batteries, where the young chicks and chickens die before reaching the age of maturity of about sixteen weeks. This creates a constant supply of feed for the maggots, and of course plenty of work for the commercial mincing machine!

Another point that I found of interest was that the flies don't 'blow' so well during periods of low pressure, and also the ammonia created by that initial influx of 400 gallons to one pit at the start of a hatch, means the smell can travel low across the surrounding fields and lie in the hollows.

All anglers will realise that flies don't lay coloured maggots. Humans make the maggots turn all the colours that fashions dictate, and one of the most popular is red. This is achieved at the farm by scattering a pink dye over the chicken carcasses. Would you believe this is the same dye as that used in the production of Blackpool rock? The maggots then eat the chicken and the dye together, although they have to be fed the dye for the entire five days they are growing in the pit.

Going back to the low pressure conditions. It was interesting to learn that the flies don't 'blow' as well in times when the weather consists of low pressure areas. Generally the fish are more active then, yet the maggots in the pits rise to the top of the feed and don't

Facing page

Top left: The flies that produce the maggots: the largest on the left is the bluebottle, followed by the smaller greenbottle, the common housefly and the menace of all maggot farms, the Horace fly.

Middle left: Several tons of dead chickens are delivered for the maggot feed; care has to be taken when handling the decomposing bodies.

Top right: In order to break the chickens down, they are minced in a commercial mincing machine.

Bottom: There are 250,000 bluebottles in this fly house alone. The shelves at the sides are covered in raw cane sugar. The sheets of newspaper hanging like washing are for the flies to clean themselves on, while the rotten pouting is laid on the floor on plastic sheets. The window is partially blackened.

31

grow so fast as in a high pressure weather system.

The statistics in the production of this maggot farm are really quite amazing. In the peak season of June and July their output rises to something around 1,000 gallons of maggots per week. From that total they have to extract some from the pits to go back up on the shelves as casters in the flyhouses to replenish the stock of breeding flies. Also, they turn out around fifty gallons of casters a week, with both caster and maggot production tailing off slightly as the autumn approaches. In the height of the season they can also use in the region of sixteen tons of dead chicken . . . every single week. For the flies to 'blow' on they use around one ton of rotten fish a week up in the flyhouses. Apparently the juices in a fish are far more nutritional than the chicken, which results in a maximum egg laying capacity. Rodney puts the hatch rate on pouting as up over 90 per cent, compared with chicken.

In summertime the air temperature is sufficient to keep the temperature in the flyhouses well up, but in the winter, when only a few flyhouses are in operation they have to be heated to 70 °F to keep those water droplets on the ceiling and thereby the humidity level high.

Three different species of fly can be used to produce the maggots that the angler uses for his hookbait or loose feed: the largest white maggots come from the bluebottle, pinkies come from the greenbottle, which is a slightly smaller fly, and has a very slight natural pink colour, and the squatts, the tiny white maggots used as

Facing page

Top left: This is a 'blow' or egg-lay; thousands of eggs are laid on just one piece of pouting. From here the sheets of plastic are taken down to the pits where they are covered to keep the eggs warm and enable them to hatch.

Middle left: Once hatched out, the maggots eat their way through the minced chickens that are forked into the pit.

Top right: When the maggots are a marketable size the minced chicken is forked into suspended bread baskets where the maggots wriggle through the holes in the bottom, leaving the partially-eaten chicken carcasses in the basket.

Bottom right: Now the maggots are graded out of the pits and into containers.

Bottom left: The maggots are stored in the refrigeration room until they are delivered to the tackle dealers.

feed, are the product of the common housefly. Rodney only uses the bluebottle, which being the larger of the maggot producers is more popular with anglers. They don't run the greenbottle during the summer months because if any of them get into the flyhouse you can get a mix of different size maggots which both the angler and the shop don't want. It's only in the winter that they put through the greenbottle, because then demand for the large maggot is lower and some of the flyhouses are killed off, which leaves more space for the greenbottles to 'blow' without mixing with the bluebottle. Also during the winter many waters will fish better on small baits, and so there's a demand for smaller bait.

In all, some 40 gallons of maggots are taken from the pits each week to be used as a new stock for the flyhouses. In the summer a caster takes around three weeks to hatch into a fly under normal temperature conditions, although this can fluctuate with any change within a set temperature range. These maggots are just stored at room temperature, but they have to put an extra gallon of sawdust into each tray so there is a complete covering over them. This is due to the danger from another species of fly that can cause havoc if it takes a hold on a maggot farm. It's tiny, and is called the Horace fly.

This disgusting little creature gets into the maggot tray and lays its eggs onto the maggot's side. Then when the maggots turn into casters, the Horace fly eggs hatch out into maggots themselves and kill the caster by eating all the insides out. The general outside appearance of the caster won't look any different, until you break it open to discover nothing but tiny Horace fly maggots inside. A sort of maggot within a maggot! When these stock casters are one day from hatching they are refrigerated to slow down their metabolism until required. The tops of some are broken off at random to see how far advanced they are towards hatching out.

As if the Horace fly doesn't pose enough of a threat, every single tray of casters destined for the stock trays of the flyhouses has to be examined for a 'rogue' caster which comes from the blackfly. This is the worst enemy of the maggot farm for they are the same size as the bluebottle, and the maggots even look the same. But when it transforms itself into the caster stage, instead of changing to a golden brown, it becomes a horrible shrivelled up black caster that is totally unsaleable, and therefore of no use to tackle dealer or angler. The blackfly is a menace because of its ability to establish itself in the maggot farm and the difficulty of eradicating it. For a start its lifespan is twice that of the bluebottle, but it also has the ability to lay twice as many eggs. This makes checking a regular routine, because if they get into the stock caster system, it results in wasted time and loss of production. The problem with blackfly usually arises from late July on to September, and fortunately they are not about during the winter. They can fly in through the main warehouse door, and lay their eggs not up in the flyhouses but into the chicken offal in the maggot pits downstairs. Using the natural body heat from the maggots already in there, they will hatch out and are therefore indistinguishable until they reach the caster stage. Occasionally some will filter through to the tackle shop, and it's then that they are picked out again at the caster stage by people like Nigel Newport of Western Fuels Tackle.

That then is your complete guided tour of one of the most unsavoury reporting jobs I have ever done.

However, as an angler I found Rodney Dunford a mine of information and while I had to retire to a portacabin with him to conduct the interview, I did 'get right in there' with my camera, and you can see the pictures that prove it. As far as I know, and according to discussions with both Rodney and Terry, this is the most up to date detail ever published for anglers.

On the drive back home I worried if the pictures would come out. The lenses kept steaming from the heat, and I definitely felt a bit weak from the overpowering smell. My reason for worrying was that if they didn't come out that was tough . . . because I wasn't going back there!

Once the maggots have actually been produced by the maggot farm and have been delivered to your tackle dealer, they go through another stage. Obviously I assume there are some tackle shops that simply dip their pint measure straight into a tray of farm maggots and sell them to the angler, and now I can only speak for my local shop Western Fuels Tackle. Here they don't just give them to the angler. The delivery is refrigerated immediately on arrival, and Nigel starts another checking system, this time his own, to ensure that his customers get only the best of the tray of maggots or casters.

One of the best hookbaits you can use is the gozzer, the largest of the maggots. This isn't a product of the maggot farm, but is generally produced by the individual angler or private enthusiast who supplies a tackle shop specially. I say enthusiast because the gozzer is nursed and cosseted almost like a pet and is produced as follows.

A box is placed, preferably in a sunny corner, at the bottom of the garden. You keep it with only a small hole for the fly to enter. Inside the box you put bran and chicken liver or similar white meat. After you get the 'blow' or egg lay, the maggots hatch out and start eating their way through the chicken liver. Then you shake them off the meat, and place them in some new bran as the moisture from their bodies will turn the previous bran sour. Then you feed them . . . wait for this . . . on a slice of white bread soaked in milk and sprinkled with brown sugar. This is in newspaper, and you must change the paper morning and evening to prevent the bran going sour. They will eat this bread, milk and brown sugar mixture for about three days after which time they are ready for the hook. They will be pure white in colour and make a very soft maggot which is popular with both fish and fishermen. You can either feed with regular white maggots and use the gozzer on the hook, which is normal procedure for matchmen, or feed just a few gozzers as loose feed. Not many shops have a supplier of gozzers, but it is always worth asking.

One of the problems that Western Fuels Tackle and many other shops have in high summer is when both the high day temperatures, and the large number of maggots in the fridge can all combine to make the fridge motor overload. Don't forget that the maggots are not the same as keeping a pound of sausages and a few pints of milk in the fridge. The maggots are alive and therefore generate their own body temperature. Open a fridge door for even a minute and the temperature rises, which in turn makes the maggots more active, which in turn means they are generating body heat. As if the overloading on the motor isn't enough the ammonia created by the maggots builds up inside and eats the coil away, which is obviously a costly replacement. Therefore the best tackle shops have more than one fridge to ensure a constant cool temperature for the maggot stock.

While in the fridge they are kept in sawdust both to soak up this ammonia by-product and to clean them, although after my visit to the maggot farm I reckon the only thing that would clean them is a bucket of Vim and a scouring brush! Nigel takes them out of the fridge and tips the whole tray into a moving riddling machine which cleans them again to remove pieces of bone, dried skin etc. They are then put in fresh sawdust and refrigerated until the angler walks into the shop with his bait box. When they are measured out many shops put in a scoop of maize, which being a fine white powder sticks to the body and makes them look larger than they are. Drop them in the water and you see the normal size maggot appear!

That's the end of the production line for the humble maggot, and I hope you will now appreciate why, with all the different stages of production involved before you get them in your bait container, the price per pint isn't cheap.

Casters

Now on to the caster, which many anglers feel is a far superior bait, and is used mostly by match anglers to extract the larger fish of a particular species from the swim. Inside each caster is a nice juicy gunge of preformed fly, and without a doubt once a fish crushes a caster and gets a taste of all that juice, he comes back for more. As a particle bait, the caster must surely rule supreme and is a prized bait among both matchmen and pleasure anglers. Once the maggots are starting to 'turn' they stop moving, and shrink slightly into a tight cylinder shape. A general slowing down of body movement is a sure indication of the commencement of change to caster. Nigel takes the maggots and riddles them off, this time using a static riddle rather than the vibrating one. The maggots not yet in the early stage of caster will slowly wriggle through the mesh and can be used as caster the following day. From here they go on to the skinning machine, which may be a plastic shute vibrated by a machine, that bounces the casters down into a tray. The shute is moistened with water applied with a wet brush to enable any dead maggot 'skins' to stick to the plastic and thus separate them from the good caster. Nigel prefers to continually tap his hand underneath the plastic shute and process the skins from the caster at his own rate. They are then finally riddled on a static riddle again to eliminate any still live maggots, then bagged up and refrigerated until ready for use. They can be kept several days at this golden brown stage, which is the peak time to use them as hookbait and loose feed. Some people actually freeze them, killing the caster and use them with success, mostly in the north of England. But having those 'live fly' juices within the caster as a fish crushes them ensures that those fish will stay in the swim looking for more.

Casters are not dyed any colours, as that natural golden brown is the best for bigger sized fish. The white maggots from the farm can really be dyed virtually any colour you want. As mentioned previously, the maggot farm dye them red via the chicken offal on which they feed, or can even use a yellow or bronze dye via that same feed. That way the colouring is actually inside the maggot and won't come off. Some tackle shops dye from the outside, using something like Spectra dye. First the maggots are riddled to clean them from excess bran, and then they are placed in a bucket. Spectra is an alcohol-based dye which is then sprayed onto them, the alcohol evaporating and leaving the dye on the maggots. Nigel finds it better to use a little rather than a lot of dye, and to leave the maggots in the bucket for half an hour. If you leave them in too high a concentrate of the dye, they simply stretch out and die. A gold or bronze maggot is the most fashionable, especially in the winter, although my own personal preference is for plain white maggots.

There you have it. As much information surrounding the production of both maggots and casters as you could possibly want. My nostrils have been totally desensitised by that visit to the maggot farm, but I am sure you, as well as I, have learnt a great deal more about what is surely the undisputed king of baits.

Nuts, Beans, Peas and Seeds

The use of nuts and seed baits of various kinds was probably brought to the fore in the early 70s when carp anglers started using large quantities of small baits in an effort to wean fish onto their hookbaits, and off the natural feed. It was the era of the particle saturation technique, which rightly or wrongly, caught a lot of carp, some of them big fish. Species other than carp fed avidly on these newly introduced baits and roach, tench, barbel and chub all responded well to the mass introduction of seed baits.

My own initiation into nuts was at Cut Mill when it was a premier carp water. I was using textured trout pellet paste flavoured with freshwater mussel extract and was hitting plenty of tench. I had to get a 100-lb-plus net of tench for an article I had to write for one of the fishing magazines, and although I knew it was a possibility, I wasn't sure just how late the tench would feed. Even though I have fished at Cut Mill for ten years, I have still never fished an entire night session at this water. Usually I travel there after work, get there at about six o'clock and pack up by 10.30 pm—not much time to put things together— but I have caught a lot of double-figure carp there, including some 20s.

Of course the local lads all giggled in their bivvies when they saw me using trout pellets because they were supposed to have been 'blown' years previously, but a 'test' fish I did one evening soon proved them wrong. After really putting in the bait, fishing two baits close in, and concentrating the feed into a six-foot square area, by 12 pm I had nearly 50 lb of fish, which was proof enough. It also indicated that I might get the magic 'ton'.

The following evening I fished with Nigel Newport from Western Fuels Tackle, but we could only get the 'hole-in-the-hedge' road swim. In an awkward position we hit tench after tench. We took 120 lb in those hours of darkness, which I think is still something of a record, but the interesting point is that after we returned the fish, the nets at the bottom were full of tiger nuts, showing that although the tench were going crazy on pellet paste, they had also been mopping up some carp anglers' loose feed. When we examined them we discovered the nuts were only partly cooked. At that time anglers did not realise the damage partially-cooked nuts could cause fish, but it is now known that they can kill if not cooked sufficiently. Although professional carp anglers always cook their baits properly, it was the youngsters trying to emulate their heroes' feats, who introduced large quantities of partially cooked nuts into the water and who were the cause of the clubs, on finding dead stock fish, having to ban the use of nuts.

But *cooked* nuts, flavoured and introduced on a reasonable scale will always catch fish, and are therefore worth mentioning within these pages. Most nuts contain a very high proportion of protein, and therefore fall within the theory of Fred Wilton that carp require a balanced diet. Some of the nuts used successfully are as follows: tiger nuts, peanuts, maples, cashew nuts and walnuts.

You can also use beans and peas: chick peas, 'tic' peas, tinned baked beans, broad beans and kidney beans. Of all these probably the safest to use are the beans. These are softer in texture, larger and absorb both colouring and flavouring better than the harder nuts. Baked beans can either be washed in a strainer to get rid of the tomato sauce in which they come, or used with the sauce. Most anglers though believe that the tomato flavouring doesn't help attract the fish and so wash the beans to get rid of it. When handling the beans remember they are going to be soft because they are precooked, so take care with them. I flavour mine by putting the washed beans into a plastic bag, tipping in a cap of the relevant flavouring and rolling the beans around in the bag very gently. If you leave them in the fridge overnight, they will have absorbed most of the flavouring which in turn will have a masking effect on that tomato sauce. For the other beans simply place in a saucepan of water, bring to the boil then simmer for twenty or thirty minutes, testing by pushing a fork in them. When they are soft, strain them off into a sieve under cold water and place in a bait container or plastic bag. Put in a capful of flavouring and away you go.

As for the tiger nuts, peanuts, cashew nuts and walnuts, if you

Facing page: Small pieces of sausage meat fished close to the edge of lilies can be a great bait for tench.

In the early days of carp fishing, breadflake and floating crust accounted for the majority of catches. The author took this carp on a slow-sinking piece of flake.

Use your loaf! Still one of the best baits, but neglected by most anglers, is bread. You can use either the white soft centre as flake or slice off some crust to make cubes for floating bait. Bread can also be mashed into groundbait when stale.

Rudd have a craving for surface or slow-sinking baits like floating casters, Sugar Puffs and casters. Use them on the little-and-often basis without using groundbait if possible.

Facing page: Chub are essentially a river fish but many stillwaters now stock them—this catch was taken from a Hampshire stillwater at dawn after loose feeding Sugar Puffs to get the chub rising to the surface.

Above: The ideal water for the bloodworm angler—a slow-moving river where the technique of pole fishing allows a careful presentation of this delicate little bait.

Left: Bloodworm—a sight to warm a matchman's heart. Fished on a size 20 hook (or less) they are extremely effective for catching small fish. Most stillwater fish will feed on this bait naturally, and can often be seen rooting on the bottom, sending up clouds of mud or streams of bubbles.

Facing page: Just one tin of sweetcorn was all the author needed to take this 124-lb-plus catch of tench, bream and carp from a Hampshire gravel pit. The plastic sheeting avoids damage to the fish.

Above: Luncheon meat and big barbel go together well—cut into cubes it can be used both as loose feed for a baitdropper, or for hookbait.

Facing page: The author with one of five barbel taken on luncheon meat from Throop fishery on the Dorset Stour. The fish were spotted individually and a strike made as the fish took the bait.

Nuts, Beans, Peas and Seeds

want to retain the right to use them on your favourite waters, you must cook them—and not just partially, but cook them well. It's quite difficult to cook them so much simply because they are so hard and they absorb moisture so slowly. Place them in a saucepan of cold water or a bait container and leave them to soak overnight. Then put them on the stove and boil them, checking every so often to make sure the pan doesn't boil dry, and test the nuts occasionally with a fork to see if they're done. Some nuts will take an hour or more. You can flavour as described before, and I have even frozen batches of flavoured nuts for future use. The flavour is reduced by this, but at least you can do enough for two or three sessions at one go in the kitchen. Overcooking is said to destroy some of the nutrients contained within the nuts. A pressure cooker allows you to cook the seeds and nuts straight from the bag in an hour, but I still prefer soaking them first.

For some reason that I am unable to fathom, the darker the seed or nut, the longer is its success on a water. This can only be because of an association of colour and fish hooking during daylight hours as nothing can be seen in the way of colour at night. If the bait starts to 'blow' simply fish light coloured ones at night, and change to darker seeds for daytime fishing. In my opinion surely a dark nut can be used as an associated bait to cause fear during daylight hours, but it still seems more effective during that time.

Prebaiting with particles like nuts must be very accurate as the chances of a fish finding a single nut cast outside the baited area is remote. They work because the fish become so engrossed in their preoccupation with feeding that they lose a little of their caution, but for obvious reasons your hookbaits have to be right in the middle of that baited area. Many anglers, and this applies to bream and tench as well as carp anglers, use a swim marker to define their baited area. This marker can be a small block of polystyrene tied to some mono with a lead-free weight. The mono is rolled up around the polystyrene block and catapulted out to unravel and hit the bottom. It is retrieved

Facing page: High summer and the streamer weed in the river is at its thickest. Do not despair for the humble maggot can percolate through the weed to lure out the fish. This is a prime area for barbel and chub using maggots inside a swimfeeder to provide a constant downstream trickle of bait.

by casting over the line at the end of the session.

At night I have been using Cyalume nightsticks as marketed by the American Cyanamid company for my markers. They were originally designed for use by campers, but American anglers were quick to spot their many uses within the fishing scene. You can get them in various colours, and worked by the same principle of nylon line and a weight, they ensure you can keep your tiny hookbait well in the area of feed. It's best to rig them to stand vertically and throw the light away from the water, as they are very bright, especially the green ones and may otherwise keep fish from moving into the swim.

Some of the seed baits will germinate if kept in a damp place so keep yours in a dry spot and boil them for at least a few minutes to

Many anglers do not believe that coarse fish other than pike, have teeth. Here is evidence of the pharangeal teeth that crush hard foods like nuts and snails. The three on the right belong to 8-lb tench, the huge set in the middle to a 37lb 2-oz Hampshire carp, and the bottom left set to a 2-lb-plus roach! I obtained this framed set from a taxidermist ten years ago.

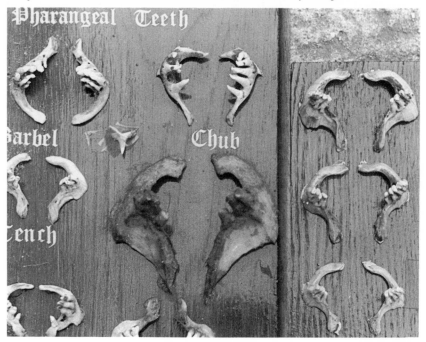

Nuts, beans, Peas and Seeds

kill off the seed germ. We don't want to see these rare plants popping up all round the lake just because somebody has 'spilt the beans'. Baits like these, when cooked, can go off and turn sour if left in the water they were cooked in. I find it better to strain then flavour and use or freeze them immediately.

Some anglers like to add their flavourings during the cooking process, even adding tins or packet soup mixes during the cooking. Personally I have found flavouring after cooking as already described works as well, although it does undoubtedly only flavour the surface. However by the time the fish has thrown it back in its mouth to crunch up with the pharangeal teeth I hope I shall have struck! As for the acquisition of these nuts and seeds there is usually a ready supply at health food shops, or some of the ethnic grocers.

Alternatively, if you really do have a craving to give nuts and seeds a good run you will save yourself a lot of money by buying in bulk from a grain and seed bulk supplier. You may find these in an agricultural newspaper or in a *Farmer's Weekly*-type of publication. You could also club together with like-minded anglers and purchase two or three sacks of different nuts, splitting both the cost and the quantity between you. I know you can save pounds like this, because I buy my trout pellets from a trout farm in 25 kg sacks. You only have to see how much weight you get in a tackle shop sample to realise the saving is enormous, and of course it allows you to be more generous in the number of baits you mix up.

Some of the nuts and seeds which have been successful in the capture of tench, bream and carp are as follows: almonds, chic peas, butter beans, kidney beans, cashew nuts, coffee beans, black-eyed beans, hazel nuts, haricot beans, maple peas, pine nuts, peanuts, sunflower seeds, pumpkin seeds, soya beans, sweetcorn, pinto beans, tiger nuts, and broad beans. Certainly more than enough to choose from when coupled with the various colouring and flavouring additives available.

Sausages

Used both in their raw state and cooked, these have long been used for barbel and carp with success, although they were most popular about twenty years ago. Anglers are always in search of that 'magic' bait which will put them on the front page of the *Angling Times* with a big catch of fish. For that reason they are quick to change to any bait that might possibly revolutionise their catch statistics. I do not belong to this school of thought and rarely change baits that are catching one fish just because fashion dictates that I change. I work on the same principle when I am fly fishing for trout, even though most anglers change patterns many times a day rather than put the pattern they have in front of a feeding fish.

Sausage meat in its raw state can either be mixed into a stiff paste by kneading in flour or better still, by adding fine white groundbait. You can then freeze it or use it the same day. Some anglers fry a flat 'pattie' of this sausage meat for about five minutes to give it both a stiffer texture (which makes it easier to cut into cubes) and to increase the fat content. I use it 'straight' myself.

Then again you have the good old-fashioned fried banger. Although I have caught barbel on sections of frankfurter and chipolatas, it's the big old fat banger that is best. Fried, cut into sections and fished on hook sizes from 10 up to a 2, they catch anything from dace to carp depending on the size you use. Never make the mistake of frying them up on the bank. That sizzling noise, together with the aroma of frying is irresistible and more than once my stock of bait has been seriously depleted by my own sampling sessions. Best to precook them, let them cool and freeze them down in plastic bags. There is no need for loose feeding on a large scale, half a dozen loose samples every so often, followed by the hookbait is sufficient.

Sausages and sausage meat are an easy bait to use, still underrated and very good for big solitary barbel.

Floaters

While most of the baits described in this book have been sinking baits, it is worth noting that floating baits can also attract certain species, though only in specific conditions. Three freshwater species spring to mind for surface fishing: In the stillwaters you have rudd and carp, while on the river scene you have the chub. Any of the following baits can be successful for these species, although it is obvious you have to scale down for the smaller rudd.

As mentioned under the section on bread, floating crust is great for surface fishing, the best crust coming from an uncut rather than a sliced loaf. To get it on the hook, insert the hook first through the white side, turn out through the top and push back through the brown crust. Because the crust will be very light, to give it some casting weight dunk it in the water for a second or two, to absorb enough water to give you the necessary weight to cast. Don't leave it in the water too long though as it will get soggy and fly off the hook when you cast.

Generally you will only get one cast from a piece of wet crust (you can't wind it in and recast), so make your first shot count and put the crust exactly where you want it. If you are fishing in a strong wind and drifting the crust down on the ripple, remember to get upwind and float it down directly below you. If you try drifting it across the wind, using a greased line it will belly and drag the crust unnaturally fast (the same principle as applies when fishing a dry fly for trout in a river). You can't afford any undue pace or drag on your bait (or fly).

If you choose to flavour your crust, the atomised flavourings mentioned in the 'Boilie' section work well. If you spray it on the white underside, the bread will absorb quite a lot and keep a flavour trail going through the water. Then too, you can make up your own floaters, like boilies, using any one of dozens of different mixes. The main problem with this though, is that if you don't follow the instructions properly, you can end up with a batch of floaters that sink!

Let's start at the beginning, where you have been to the local tackle shop and purchased the relevant base powder for your floater mix. You have emptied the powder into a dish and added the eggs, flavouring and colouring. Now here is the way to make sure your

Above left: Other than bread crust, a very acceptable floating bait is made from dog 'Chum Mixer' biscuits. Soak them for 10 minutes. Strain off all but a little water and cover with a lid. Leave for 3 hours to swell and soften. Strain off any remaining water and add flavouring as required.

Above right: On the left is a home-made baked floater. on the right are Sugar Puffs! Moistened for a minute and then strained off, they float well and catch anything from big carp to rudd. As a casting aid to this light bait you can add some green Flotabait about 2 feet up from the hook.

floaters FLOAT . . . whisk like crazy to trap as many air bubbles into the mix as possible. Think of a bar of Aero chocolate and try to get the mixture looking like that—and then it will be light enough to float. Some people prefer to whisk the colouring and flavouring straight into the egg mix then put in the powder next, but I don't think it makes too much difference, since it's all eventually whisked together anyway. Once this has been done, pour the mixture into a greased baking tin or similar receptacle, put it in a pre-heated oven and cook slowly for about an hour and a half. Just like the best cooked cakes, the inside should be slightly moist and the outside a bit rubbery. When you tip it out of the baking tin, and it has cooled, simply cut it into whatever size pieces you want.

Floaters

If you want circular baits, you should roll out your bait mixture first, but for floater fishing I don't find shape makes that much difference. Often if the carp have been hammered on round boilies on the bottom a change in size with a surface-fished bait will create a more positive take.

Rudd rise to flavoured floaters avidly, although you need to cut the sizes down to somewhere around the size of your little finger nail, and fish primarily at dawn or dusk.

An easier way to get a lot of floaters quickly is to take a trip to your local supermarker or pet food shop and buy a selection of pet biscuits that will keep you going for a session. The most popular for bulk feeding is 'Munchies', a cat food that comes in several different flavours and only needs to be soaked briefly to swell before they are ready to use. Do it this way. Tip a quarter of the packet into a large bait container. Tip in enough cold water to cover, and after 60 seconds, strain off, put the lid on and leave for several hours. The pellets will have swollen to at least double their size as they absorb the moisture and when ready should have a slightly spongy feel about them. They can be used on their own or if you want to add additional flavour, place the biscuits in a plastic bag, tip in a capful of flavouring, and rub them around inside the bag. Leave for an hour and they will all be tainted with the flavour. Simple and easy.

Another effective surface bait is Sugar Puffs, which when soaked for 15 seconds and strained off, also absorb moisture. You may need to add either a bubble float or the green 'Flotabait' to give you something extra for casting.

How about marshmallows? These don't need soaking, are very spongy and can be threaded straight onto a number 2 carp hook. They are best fished whole for carp, as once you start trying to pull smaller pieces off they stick to your fingers, you take a lick, then that's it . . . you eat the rest of the bait yourself!

Various dog biscuits and other cat mixer foods can be adapted as floaters, and in my opinion are among the more efficient baits. When fishing on a river for chub for instance, your baits are going to disappear at an alarming rate, and most people simply cannot afford to use a lot of specially-cooked floater mix which just drifts away (unlike on a lake where they only move if there is a wind). Better to find your chub swim first, then sit there running through floating 'Munchies' until you see a take. Sometimes it is possible to see a fish boil further downstream than the fish you were after, therefore indicating a trip downstream is necessary. Floaters have an advantage in that not too many anglers use them compared to bottom baits. You are giving the fish something different, which when on a hammered water, may be all you need to succeed. Aside from that the excitement of seeing a fish suck your hookbait down is far better than sleeping your way through the day or night, with the only thing to watch being an inert bobbin indicator!

Bloodworms

This is primarily the bait of the matchman, and if I say it is tiny, it really is almost microscopic! Used for the capture of small fish in fishing matches, the bloodworm when used by a competent pole angler will produce fish after fish. I personally have no use for them because the first year's fry can be taken using this bait, so it really is just a specialist matchman bait.

The bloodworm is the larvae of the gnat, and is transparent but a glistening ruby red colour. It squirms, and twists all the time and it is easy to see why it is so attractive to fish.

The acquisition of the bloodworm is both difficult and labour intensive so should your tackle shop be able to get some, expect to pay £8 for a single pint of these little wrigglers. They are gathered by an angler or collector wading out in a mud-bottomed lake using chest waders. He has a long pole with a thin, flat curved blade on the tip, not unlike those old scythes of years ago. This is drawn slowly through the mud which flows over the top of the blade, hopefully leaving lots of bloodworms sticking to it. The worms are then wiped off and put in a container. This scraper for collecting is not rigid, but is slightly pliable and made from rustproof metal. An average-size bloodworm blade would be about two inches wide, $1/16$th of an inch thick and perhaps 18 inches long. The container into which the collector puts the bloodworms (remember he is up to his armpits in water) has a mesh lining. This fine mesh cloth is dipped into the lake to make it wet and then used to strain the bloodworms.

Storage is just as time consuming as collecting, for the bloodworms need to be kept damp. This can be done by storing them in a shallow dish with just enough water to cover them. I have heard that rain water is preferred to tap water as the chlorine slows up their movements. When you want to take them on your session, change them to a plastic bait container lined with damp newspaper, with either damp moss, sand or even tea leaves in the bottom. Cover again with a piece of damp newspaper. Some anglers prefer keeping them in just a couple of folds of damp newspaper lined with peat. They do keep better like this, but remember that peat also dries out quicker too, and since the object of the exercise is to keep them moist, always check the peat is kept damp. The cooler they are the better, so the garage or an outside shed is the best place for them. In winter you can reckon on keeping them for about two weeks, but the warmer weather or summer will see them lively only for a week, which isn't very long after all that effort!

The bloodworm is used as the hookbait, but tiny bloodworms, or 'jokers' as they are called, are used as the loose feed, and are generally sent into the swim in pellets of groundbait or black earth with a high peat content. The jokers are more prolific wherever there is a high sewage effluent, and their collection would certainly not put them high on my list of priorities.

While I said that this bait is almost exclusively used by the serious matchman, mostly canal anglers on the pole, I have heard of bream being taken on them. They are the natural diet of all fish, except the predators, and if you see a tench bubbling, or a carp sending up clouds of mud you can be fairly sure it is up to its eyes in mud and filtering the bloodworm into its throat.

The reason you don't catch big fish on bloodworm is probably due to hook size, and the fact that your tiny hookbait doesn't exactly stand out with the billions of other bloodworms in the water. You need a fine wire hook with a low barb to prevent bursting them, the best way to hook them being to place one on the tip of your finger and to insert the hookpoint through the thick dark segment end. This allows it to wriggle better, although years ago, specialist roach anglers used to whip them on to the hook using a fine red silk. You may want to try collecting your own as an experiment, but make sure you take someone with you, as there is always danger when chest wading in soft muddy water.

Luncheon Meat

This must be one of the best 'clean' baits to use, and it is used almost exclusively for big chub and barbel. Luncheon meat can either be bought fresh from a delicatessen counter or tinned. Whilst the tinned meat is useful to store, I have found the fresh luncheon meat to be better at staying on the hook.

If you do buy it fresh don't get it sliced. You want something like a 1-lb block or roll that you can cut in half. Freeze one half down for future use, and keep the other in the fridge for use that same day or the next. The disadvantage of tinned meat is that it has a higher water and jelly content that makes it less satisfactory on the hook. However it still catches fish.

Luncheon meat is successful due to its high fat content (the kind in the tins may have a higher fat content than the fresh) and this can be increased even more by trying the following tip. Melt some fat or lard in a frying pan on a low heat, and when it has only just melted drop in your pre-cut cubes of fresh luncheon meat. Spoon the fat over the meat so it covers all sides and remove from the heat. When it cools you will find a thin film of fat covering the cubes which in my experience makes it more attractive to barbel and chub.

If you purchase a tinned variety that turns out to be soft, you must cut it into cubes of hookbait size and keep it in the fridge overnight. By doing this it will develop a tougher, dark outer skin which allows it to be cast better, and also prevents smaller fish like dace and roach nibbling away at it.

Whereas bit baits like cheese will go hard in the winter floodwater, luncheon meat will still stay soft enough for good hook penetration.

A tinned variety of meat worth trying in the really big hook sizes, say number 2 and upwards for barbel and carp, is chopped pork and ham. Some anglers even dip this into one of the ham flavoured concentrates available from the tackle shops. This does seem like overkill however, and the only improvement I have found to be successful is dipping the cubes into warm lard as described.

Cheese

Cheese is a firm favourite of many anglers, yet it is still not used as widely as it deserves. Three types of cheese baits can be used for hookbaits. The first is a cheesepaste made from flour, water and grated cheese. This is kneaded until a firm rubbery texture has been achieved with the consistency of a paste. An alternative and very acceptable cheesepaste can also be made by kneading bread and a little water together, then adding a capful of cheese concentrate flavouring—which certainly gives it a pungent odour. Fish, especially in a river flood in winter, locate their food by smell, and cheesepaste is especially useful in the cold. If you don't use an additional flavouring, but still want a very soft paste then use something like Dairylea cheese. This comes in soft form already, and can be stiffened up slightly by adding some fine white groundbait and mixing together with damp hands. You'll probably need a careful cast to prevent it coming off, and with larger hook sizes (around number 2), you can place a tiny section of matchstick in the bend of the hook and mould the paste around that, to keep it on. If done properly, even a soft piece of cheese paste can be cast as far as sixty yards.

The second type of cheese bait is the hard cheddar-type cheese. You can buy it in bulk, cut it into smaller blocks and freeze it, but the actual freezing process dehydrates the cheese and makes it crumbly. Anglers often use this block cheese in cubes or chunks like luncheon meat, but I have enjoyed greater success by breaking off a piece, squeezing it between my fingers a few times, then moulding it around the hook. Fished on a size 8 or 10, a thumbnail-sized piece of cheese like this will take everything from barbel and chub in a fast-flowing river, to roach and tench in stillwater.

Cheese is probably my most productive chub bait, especially when fished in conjunction with the freelining technique. There is little need for prebaiting which is probably just as well, as most of the cheeses are over £1 for a pound in weight. Some of the more expensive cheeses I have tried are Edam and Red Leicester, but still the best is the cheapest mild English cheddar.

A single day's chub fishing on the Avon or Stour will usually see me using only 1¼lb of English cheddar, and being home produced as against an imported variety, it is relatively cheap. Generally speaking, if you can spot and stalk a chub, whether individually or in a shoal, that first cast should get you a fish. If it doesn't it's likely to be because they have been fished for with maggots and casters, after which you may not get a take until the light has failed. It may be worth throwing half a dozen pellets in just to see if you can start them feeding, but failing that, rest them for an hour then try again. You can often get a take first cast.

The third type is cheese flavouring mixed in with groundbait. This can be useful when chub fishing on the float, and it can pull the barbel in as well. Tiny pieces float-fished through a baited area have given me many roach topping the pound mark that would look at nothing else. Cheese is a prime big-fish bait that is still not used too much and is consequently effective.

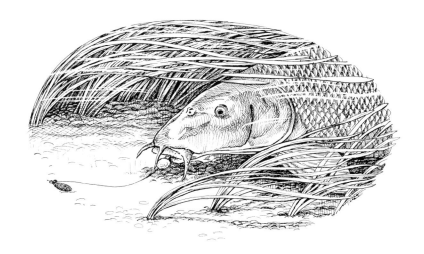

Slugs

Slugs sound like a bait from yesteryear but they can be used to good effect when stalking chub in clear water on hard-fished waters. Slugs are best obtained either from under stones and fallen trees, or simply in the back garden on wet, mild nights after a short dry spell. I keep them in a plastic bait container with some grass cuttings in, and obviously with the lid on. They can be fished whole on a big single hook, or as advised by the chub anglers of years ago, 'have their bellies split to reveal the white inside'. I don't really think you need do this, and I have taken chub on both split and unsplit baits. The answer lies in using a longish tail on your leger link to give the chub time to take it properly. I have not had any real success with them on the float, but quivertipped in a slack, or in a deep run in classic 'snaggy' chub country they may pick up the extra bonus fish when all else fails.

Chips

Chips were something I used on chub down on the Royalty fishery of the Hampshire Avon when I ran out of cheese. It was getting dark; just that time of day when I knew I was going to get more bites. My wife came back from the town with bangers and chips and I rammed the bangers down in three gulps and looked at those huge fatty chips. I remembered dipping the luncheon meat in fat to give them a good coating, and looking at the state of the chips they didn't need any further dips into anything. They were the big chunky variety, the thickness of your finger, so I broke a section off, baited up, ate the rest and cast out. The chip disappeared from view and I concentrated on watching the bow in the line. It tweaked, I struck and minutes later landed a good chub. I baited with another chip section, ate the rest and cast out. A missed bite. By the time I had used all the chips I had taken three chub, all round the 3-lb mark, and missed more. I contemplated a reduction of vinegar or the addition of salt, but there was no need, as in the following couple of weeks I took more chub on fatty chips.

So there's yet another bait for you to try, and if you can deep fry a load back home they really do represent a good cheap bait!

Wheat

Wheat is not a bait used much nowadays. Although it could be described mainly as a roach bait, it is also an alternative for you to try on other species. If you use wheat you are sure to bypass the smaller fish and winkle out the better ones, and this is especially so with roach and rudd.

Preparation is by soaking the wheat grains for several hours in cold water, draining off the water (there is no extra flavour in the water from the grains) and putting the grains in a saucepan of water. Bring to the boil for five minutes, then turn down to simmer. Once the grains have swollen up and split they should be washed in a sieve under the cold tap and they are then ready for hookbait. Wheat strikes me as a fairly bland bait, but used in conjunction with a bread-based groundbait it can be effective. You can increase its effectiveness by adding some of the modern flavourings—and don't forget that wheat has good absorption should you wish to colour it. For roach and bream the only real flavour and colouring combination I know of is to dye the grains red and flavour them with vanilla. You can also cook the wheat grains by the vacuum flask method as described in the hempseed section.

It has been suggested that the success of boiled wheat is due to its resemblance to a pea mussel, but surely that means every other bait must resemble something? I think the fish take wheat simply because it is soft and edible. Two grains set on a size 10 or 12 hook should be sufficient for the floatfisherman, with more being used on a larger size hook by anyone wishing to leger. Like hempseed, the bend of the hook is pushed into the split on the husk caused by boiling.

Facing page: The author's favourite bait for stalking chub in clear water is cheese. Using either Cheddar or Edam, just squeeze once or twice before moulding on to the hook.

64

Above: The author unhooks a 4lb-plus River Stour chub. Cheese nearly always liphooks the fish whereas maggots and worms can sometimes result in throat hooking.

Facing page: The author slides a Hampshire Avon chub over the net. Freelined cheese gave the author his biggest catch of chub in a day . . . over 80lb with individual fish over 4lb.

Above: The tiniest seed bait is hemp. On the right is the paler uncooked seed, while on the left, proper cooking gives you a jet black shiny seed with a splash of white where the seed has burst.

Facing page: Hempseed comes into its own during the winter months when it is used as a feed to caster, which is the hookbait. Do not overfeed but throw in on the little-and-often basis.

Left: Big lobworms are especially good for trout, carp, salmon, tench and chub. Unfortunately small perch and bootlace eels like them too!

Above: A nice earthworm can be fished in sections, singly or in bunches.

Bottom left: Red worms are excellent for catching bream.

Bottom right: Brandling used either on its own or as a cocktail bait is also good for bream.

Facing page: Over 200lb of bream (the largest single fish was 5lb) caught on brandlings.

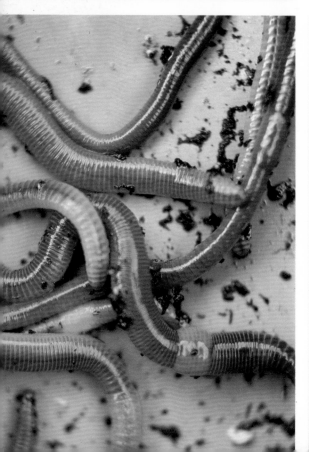

Caddis

Larvae are much easier to obtain than bloodworms and are an offbeat bait that can give success when others fail. Being a 'natural' bait it might seem strange that I am calling it offbeat, but it is meant in terms of how often it is used by the angler. The fish eat them avidly enough in their natural state, so why not put one on the hook and isolate it from the bottom?

Finding them is not difficult if you know where to look. Wading in a shallow stream and turning over the stones should locate some, as will searching the bark of sunken branches caught on the bottom or in backwaters and eddies. They tuck themselves into the cracks of rotting bark and the cases they build around themselves can make spotting them an art in itself. Once known as 'stick bait' due to its resemblance to pieces of twig, the caddis grub used to be eased out of its case and hooked lightly, just once through the end. Modern underwater photography has shown us that this is not necessary, as a feeding fish simply wolfs the lot down, casing and all! Presumably the pharangeal teeth are used for crushing the stones and other debris which the caddis has built as a shell.

One way to extract them from the shell should you wish is to squeeze the case where the tail is and grab the head that emerges at the other end.

No need to loose feed with them, just a single caddis floatfished or freelined down a run in the streamer week will usually be taken by a roach, dace, or chub.

Facing page: With the advent of commercially-made boilie baits came a boom in carp, tench and barbel catches.

Mussels

Mussels are one of the old favourites for tench and carp fishing. There are two types to try: the freshwater swan mussel which grows to about six inches long, and the sea mussel which is considerably smaller. While I know the sea mussel will catch freshwater fish, I confess that I have yet to hear of a freshwater swan mussel taking a sea fish. It must be a possibility though. Sea mussels can easily be obtained from—yes, the sea—or better still if you live inland, the local fishmonger. A pint of mussels is easily enough for a bit of groundbaiting and plenty for the hook.

The freshwater species can be taken by throwing out a fine wire rake with the ends bent back in like cat's claws and retrieving it over the muddy bottom of a lake. The easiest way to extract either a fresh sea or freshwater mussel from its shell is by boiling. However this cooked mussel has not the same juices as a raw one so here's how to get a nice gunky mussel out of its shell without having to cook it. First take a 3-lb coal hammer and a vice (sorry, only joking). To do it properly, hold the mussel in your left hand, insert a knife (preferably blunt) and sever the mussel foot at the hinge of the shell. Ease the shell open, and slide the mussel meat out by slipping the knife against the inside of the shell until you have the entire mussel in your palm. I find the best way to put a freshwater swan mussel on is to use a large hook, around number 2, hook it once through the mussel and whip the rest with a piece of elasticated thread. This is taking a tip out of the sea angler's book, and it stops this very soft bait flying off during the cast.

If you fish at night you'll soon find that eels have a liking for a nice blob of mussel meat, and I would advise striking quite early as any fish seems to get this meat down its neck as quickly as possible. There is also a mussel extract available, and this is first class for tench when mixed with trout pellets into a paste. It seems to get a very early fish or two, so I assume that the smell exuding from a swan mussel diffuses into the surrounding area quite quickly.

Mussels are not a bait that I use frequently, but as a bait that is good for both tench and eels, it should be included in any bait book.

Shrimps and Prawns

These are two sea baits but because both are very good for chub I have included them. Some years ago, maybe as many as twelve now I come to think of it, I had a phase of trying to catch salmon from the Hampshire Avon. I went through the dyed-prawn phase, the lacerated lobworm and the teal-blue-and thingy, but although the salmon were not impressed, the chub certainly were! In fact they were so interested in small brown shrimps that I stopped trying to catch a salmon and caught the chub instead.

Small brown shrimps are obtained from the local fishmonger and aren't expensive for a half pint, which is about all you are going to need for a session. You can use them peeled, which facilitates early striking, or you can use them with casing, legs, whiskers and all. I prefer the latter, inserting the hook in at the tail, threading as much of the shrimp as I can up and around the bend and bringing the hookpoint out just underneath what I would say is the throat. When legered on the bottom the hookpoint is facing downstream, but when retrieved slowly in a river, the shrimp is facing the right way i.e.. tail into the current. So many chub tried to grab the shrimp when I started bumping it back upstream, that it really is a bait to keep on the move.

Particular attention should be paid to weir pools where there is a boiling heavy current to allow you to either trundle the shrimp around on a leger, or simply trot it in the runs between streamer weed under an Avon float. If you use the float don't forget to delay the strike for a second or two as it is a big bait, and it may be a pound chub tugging at it instead of a four pounder. With no need to loose feed, I just work my way through swims using them one at a time.

Prawns, on the other hand need to be peeled if you want to connect on the strike. A prawn with whiskers and casing is not too large for a chub, but anglers very often strike too early as Mr Chub eats his way up it. Better to fish it peeled, the only problem being that after peeling half a dozen for bait the desire to eat them yourself becomes almost overpowering! Rig as you would do a brown shrimp, in through the tail and out near the throat.

Bread

In its various forms the humble loaf of bread has probably accounted for more big fish over the last century than any other bait, and even though it has currently fallen out of fashion with the advent of boilies, seeds, and maggots, nevertheless it is still a bait worth using now and again. As I wouldn't have thought its scent was very great, it must surely be its soft texture and visibility that make fish keen to take it. While most of our bread today comes ready cut, I still find the best texture comes from the inside of those crusty cottage loaves. The main problem is it tastes so good I often end up eating half the bait supply before I've had chance to use it.

Three basic baits can be made from a loaf of bread. The crust floats and small thumbnail-sized pieces are excellent for rudd fishing close to rushes or floating weeds. Then there is that lovely fluffy centre, or flake which can be used by simply pinching a piece onto a hook and casting out. Finally there is breadpaste—one of the oldest baits, but still effective for tench and big roach.

To make breadpaste, the entire inside white of the loaf is put in a teacloth, rolled up and soaked in water. The surplus water is then squeezed out, and the bread is squeezed and drained until it has formed into a paste. Some anglers like to stiffen the mixture up with the addition of flour. A pellet of white breadpaste on a small hook still catches roach, but it can be enhanced by the modern flavourings.

For the match angler wanting to use a bread punch, in which a predetermined size of flake is pushed onto the hook, the uncut loaf is unsuitable. Especially for the smaller bread punch sizes, a slice from a medium cut loaf will do admirably, and it is easy to push the breadpunch into each slice. Another method, that I saw used only recently—by a barbel angler in search of double-figure fish from the Dorset Stour—was this. He lay a slice of cut bread on a piece of plastic then sprayed some flavouring straight onto the slice. His bread punch, a large model, was pushed in, the flavour sprayed breadflake hooked on, and then cast out. All this was done without the bait being touched or tainted by the human hand.

An advantage of using breadflake is that it is a slow sinking bait that can be fished over weed, unlike the heavier beans, seeds and maggots that quickly sink to the bottom. If you do fish with a sinking

76

paste bait it is really easy to add a piece of crust to the bend of the hook which will slow down the bait and let it rest on top of the bottom debris, rather than sinking from view.

The pastes made up by anglers years ago in the pursuit of roach were almost entirely bread based, and it's interesting to note that varying shades of red were achieved by the addition of Rhodamine, Chrysoidine or vermillion. Yellow was achieved by the addition of saffron or chrome yellow. While the hazards of using Chrysoidine have been documented before, there is no doubt that good use could be made of the 'Safe' colourings and flavourings currently available on the market.

Sweetcorn

I think that sweetcorn has to be one of the most productive baits of the last decade—whether used for big single fish like carp, or for bags of fish like roach and bream. A bright gold in colour, sweet to taste, soft in texture and of a size that precludes the capture of too many small fish, you couldn't ask for a better all-round bait.

Sweetcorn comes mainly from the USA where it is grown in abundance, and is cooked and eaten while still on the cob. Eaten hot and with a knob of butter, it is superb. By comparison the corn grains in the tins from the local supermarket are poor—but they are good for tench, roach, carp, barbel and chub, and I advise every angler to give them a try. For roach you really need just a single grain, while tench will take two or three, and the carp and barbel several grains on a size 6 hook or larger.

At one stage on the Royalty at Christchurch, maggots were banned, and it was then that corn started to be used as a particle saturation bait. We enjoyed a lot of success using sweetcorn as a 'string of pearls', where as many as six or eight grains were threaded over the point of the hook, round the bend up the shank and over the eye. As a particle saturation bait for carp it is superb, and then it is used in it's natural state without any additives. It is a bait for early success, and I attribute this to the attractive qualities of that bright gold colour. By the same token it is a bait that can lose its success rate quickly if everybody starts using it as the fish seem to associate its gold colour with being hooked before! If this happens the answer then lies in either dying the grains a different colour, and/or flavouring them as well.

Two easy ways to buy sweetcorn are either frozen or in tins. If you are going to get through quite a bit it's cheaper to buy the bulk 3-lb frozen packs, but if you only use it on the odd session you may as well stick to the tinned variety which is ample for hookbait and loose feed for a single session. Sweetcorn has a tendency to go off really quickly (especially in warm weather), once the tin is opened, but you can slow this down a bit by draining off the juice from the tin. Don't waste the juice however, but pour it into your groundbait mix. I then fill a bait container up with water and put the corn grains in that. If you have a cold box, then that is even better, for it is the temperature more than anything that makes the corn go sour. Don't worry, you'll know by the smell when it has gone off—in the summer it's usually the next day!

As for dyes, both black and red are good colours to try, with the Catchum colourings being among the best to try. So too are the 200-ml bottles of Spectra dye. Their gold colouring enhances the naural colour of the corn and was a popular colouring for matchmen to mix in their groundbait during the winter months when they were hookbaiting with bronze maggots. Of course the fish may not see the same colours as we do, but at least it would appear a different colour to them, even if in shades of grey, and maybe reduce that fear factor.

Sweetcorn is also a great cocktail bait, especially when fished at night. Then of course you don't get any colour at all, but the attractions of the sweet flavour from corn, and those 'excitement' juices from a worm all combine to give good confident baits later in the season when things start to get hard.

A few tins of sweetcorn in the cupboard are always a good standby; sweetcorn is a cheap bait to buy, and easy to use.

Hempseed

This tiny black seed must surely be one of the best 'feeds' in the business. One of the premier roach baits of the thirties, it proved to be so successful at some big river venues that it was banned. In fact the Hampshire Avon at Christchurch and Dorset Stour at Throop still operate a ban on its use. Its vast success with the early roach fishermen, who incidentally hammered the fish even in bright sunny summer conditions, was thought to be due to the fact that the tiny hempseed resembled a freshwater snail or mussel. It was thought by some to be so successful that fish would refuse to look at any other bait once it was introduced. Others thought it contained some sort of natural drug that drove the fish wild. Tests have proved that hempseed as a food for fish is not a drug. At one stage a Government publication recommended hempseed for fattening fish in ponds so there is little doubt in my mind that banning its use is wrong.

Some said that hempseed fouled the bottom and then started growing underwater. Fortunately the Royal Botanic Society stepped in and confirmed that once boiled, the germ was killed and could not possibly grow. In fact hempseed required a hot dry climate to grow, so it would need a botanical miracle for a hempseed plant to sprout from a river or lake bed!

There may have been those anglers unfamiliar with the method of feeding (which was on the little and often basis) who by throwing large handfuls of cooked hempseed into their swim, merely sent the fish to the bottom where they stayed to eat to their heart's content.

Belgian refugees established hempseed as a good roach bait during the First World War, and thereafter it was quickly used to devastating effect by the roach fishermen at Richmond. One report said that at least 25 roach 2 lb plus came from the Thames in the 1931–2 season, which illustrates how effective it can be in the right hands. It's a fast sinking bait which makes it easier to judge when feeding the fast water that roach, dace, barbel and chub love.

Its use as a hookbait today is still popular, as the hard shuck of the outer casing makes it difficult for the hook to penetrate. Better if the need arises, to use a fine wire hook and push the bend of the hook into the white part of the seed, which splits through the cooking process. Primarily used by floatfishermen, it is best to use either a self-cocking float or a twist of copper wire to prevent the fish nipping at the shot and thereby giving 'false' bites. Today the humble hempseed is used with the swimfeeder when anglers are fishing casters and maggots, for it definitely contains something that holds the fish hard in the swim.

There are a couple of ways to cook it, but first remember it may not be worth the hassle unless you, like many anglers, enjoy making your own baits. Many tackle shops now stock ready-frozen hemp in pre-packed bags, already pre-cooked. All you have to do is drop the block into a bait tin of water and wait until it thaws. But it's much cheaper to cook your own, and of course there is nothing to stop you freezing down your own batches for future use. First you need to soak your hempseed overnight in a bucket or saucepan full of cold water. This softens the seed and makes for a shorter boiling time. Next day strain off the surplus water into another container for use when mixing up your groundbait. There is an oil inside the hempseed and it may be this that attracts the fish. Top the saucepan up with water, bring to the boil quickly then simmer for fifteen minutes until the kernels split to reveal that white slash which is to be your hookhold if required. This is a sign that the seed is cooked. If you don't pre-soak the seed, it may take about 40 minutes to cook properly. Again, don't waste that juice but drain it off into a container for use with your groundbait mix.

If you are deciding to fish it on the hook as a single grain remember there are now plastic imitation hempseeds available at tackle shops, which save baiting up every time you strike.

Other tricks are to use a length of black rubber tubing with a white spot painted on it. Take care to cut this tubing to the same size as the other seeds. A tiny piece of bootlace cut to size and white tipped will do the same job, and years ago a glass bead painted black with a white gloss tip was used.

Most anglers today will be using hempseed as an additive and attractant when swimfeeding for barbel and chub, and it's also possible to buy crushed hemp as a powder to mix in with your groundbait. Remember that it can, like sweetcorn, go sour in a couple of days, so if you take a batch from the freezer and don't use it all, be sure to rinse the seeds to moisten them before refreezing.

Another way to cook hempseed is by thermos flask. Fill a flask about a third full of seed then top up the remainder with boiling water. Screw on the top and leave for about six hours. This can be done the day you decide to go fishing, or even the night before, thus saving you time if you want to take advantage of good weather conditions. Remember that those seeds are covered with boiling water, so don't just tip straight out into the palm of your hand! Always keep your cooked seed wet. If it dries out in the sun it will float and may pull the fish away downstream from you.

I personally can't see the fact that it looks like a freshwater snail or mussel is good reason for its uncanny-fish holding properties: I have had tremendous catches by using the new crushed hemp in with my groundbait when there is no mussel or snail resemblance at all. I feel it is the oil itself which is released by the seed that attracts the fish, and when one of the bait manufacturers comes up with a pure hempseed oil concentrate, then I will be among the first to give it a thorough trial.

The fashion today is to use hempseed as a bottom fish holder, but it can be used as surface loose feed provided tares are used as the hookbait.

Tares

The use of tares as a bait was largely brought about because of the difficulty anglers experienced in keeping, or even putting the tiny hempseed on to their hooks. Tares on the other hand were a larger seed altogether which some said sorted out the larger fish, but really made hooking a little more easier. By loose feeding hemp and using a cooked tare on the hook the roach revival began, and even chub and barbel were caught on them. The whole of the tare is soft when properly cooked, whereas the hempseed only has that white split into which a hookbend can be pushed. With hempseed, if you strike the seed is off and you have to rebait again. This system of fishing is designed for hot summer days when very little else is going to feed and you can't risk crashing in the balls of groundbait. It is very easy to overfill the fish with tares, possibly even more so than the hemp, so anything that goes in must be done very sparingly.

A few tackle dealers will cook and freeze down tares for their customers, but many find it more trouble than hemp and therefore leave it to the angler. Tares can emit quite a smell when cooking, so the advance cold soak overnight is recommended to keep the cooking time down—especially if you want your wife's permission to use the kitchen again! Add a tablespoon of bicarbonate of soda to this overnight soaking as it helps the tares keep that black finish and stops them going a dull brown. There doesn't seem to be the same oil content in a tare as there is in hempseed so I tip the soak water away rather than keep it.

To cook, put the tares in a saucepan, fill with water and add a little sugar; it is supposed to give them an added sheen, but I wouldn't worry too much if you forget. What you shouldn't forget though is one of the flavouring concentrates that are used by the carp boys. A teaspoon of this makes both the tares and the kitchen smell a bit sweeter—maple syrup or strawberry flavours being my favourites. Check after about ten minutes of gentle boiling to see if they are turning soft. If necessary reduce the heat to a simmer and check regularly. When soft enough for use as a hookbait they are cooked. Never strain them straight under a cold tap though which causes them to split. Better to let them cool off on their own or run them under warm water. You can also cook them using the flask technique (see Hempseed) but don't put in too many as they tend to expand more than hemp. About half a flask full of tares topped up with boiling water will do.

These seeds can also be flavoured when they are cold, rather than during the boiling process. Simply dip a wipe of cotton wool in your flavouring, rub it round your bait tin, add the tares and then give a good shake around—preferably with the lid on! Throw in the cotton wipe as well, and you will find your tares ready for the hook and tainted perfectly with your required flavour.

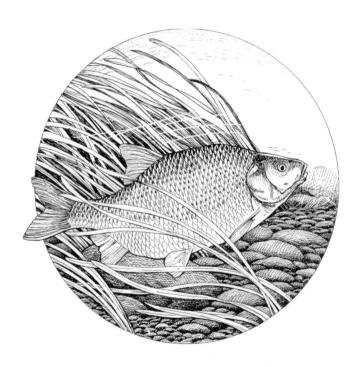

Worms

Possibly one of the most underrated modern baits is the humble worm—not so much when used on its own, but when liquidised in a food processor it can make one of the best baits for a wide variety of species. Once liquidised, tip the resultant goo out of the mixer, straight into a two-pint bait tin and after adding flour and water, mix into a stiff paste. Then keep wetting your fingers and kneading the paste until it reaches the consistency you require. Nothing could be cheaper or simpler than that, yet many anglers still fail to take advantage of the excellent attracting properties of worm juices. Surely you have tried snapping the tip off a worm and letting the drips fall into a tank of aquarium fish? The fish go absolutely bananas looking for the source of the smell. Of course making this paste could turn out a whole lot more expensive than expected if you fail to wash the food processor out and your wife sues for divorce!

The worm in its natural state can be extracted from the earth by several means—the least easy of which is to find yourself on the wrong end of a fork.

Worms love damp, warm places so the manure heap is the ideal place to look for those tiger striped brandlings. A small worm, they are deadly when floatfished for sea trout and must be fished on a fine wire hook. Certainly too good to chop up and put in the groundbait, they are initially a river bait, thrown in as loose feed, with a single frantic wriggler on the hook, for dace, chub, roach and the legendary perch. Brandlings work well as a coloured water bait, though whether this is due to the scent given off from the manure heap in which they live, or the extra frantic wriggling they do, I don't know. I know some older anglers believe it is the smell of the manure in which they live, and I have heard of men loose feeding the manure itself into a river in flood swim. When a ball of this unsavoury mixture hits the surface it makes a sort of clanging noise: 'DUNG!'

Next in line size-wise comes the redworm. Found in damp areas with plenty of leaf mould, they will be just under the surface, and require little digging. They are excellent in the groundbait, and even better legered on the bottom. They are a particularly good tench bait, though almost any species will take them. Three or four fished with a swimfeeder of groundbait can really cane the bream. Redworms are probably my favourite worm: they're easy to get, and a real fish catcher.

Then we come to the largest of the three worms used by anglers, the lobworm. A lob can measure from four inches long, to a real strangler of six inches plus. The best lobs come from cricket and golfing greens, but the owners don't take too kindly to having that expensive turf dug up by a fork. Obtain permission first, then on a damp night creep across the green in a pair of carpet slippers and quietly shine a torch about. You should find plenty of lobworms half out of their holes. Don't yank them out but do it carefully as described: swiftly, but smoothly grab the worm near the base of the hole and rather than pull it, just wait for its muscles to relax and then you can slide it out. This must be the best way to collect a large number of lobs, although in very dry warm weather any sort of worm is going to be deeper in the ground to get at that cool moisture.

Another way to extract lobworms is by filling a watering can with water and washing up liquid (again the night should be damp so the worms are relatively near the surface), then watering a square patch of your lawn with the mixture. When you go back a couple of hours later you should find masses of them stretched out on the top ready to be just picked up.

Lastly, to get enough worms for hookbait in difficult, dry weather, try getting a couple of old doormats (the bristly type) and turning them upside down in a dark corner of the garden. Keep them well soaked and you should have some small worms underneath in a couple of days. There won't be a lot, but enough for a few hookbaits.

Worms can be kept a long time, provided you look after them. Scouring them in damp moss is the old-fashioned, but still the best way to keep them fresh and strong. A good lively worm has an iridescent sheen to it. Additives to the damp moss used to be milk, or even red brickdust which was used as a colouring agent in years past. Some anglers put a couple of drops of flavouring in with them, but I leave mine as they are. The worm's natural scent is obviously biologically strong, and I see no point in masking that with another flavouring agent. By pulling out any dead worms, and keeping the moss damp (with rainwater, not tap water), you can keep them for

Worms

The best place to dig worms is in a damp, moist place. A heap of rotting leaves is good for lobworms and redworms, while an old manure heap will give you all the brandlings you require. The centre and bottom of the manure heap is best. Keep the worms in damp moss and store in a cool place until needed.

several weeks if stored in a cool and dark place.

Should you wish for a constant supply of worms then you must build your own wormery which is a grand name for an enclosed compost heap kept wet. Worms need something to eat in the shape of leaves, grass cuttings, tealeaves or torn up newspaper, and can be kept almost indefinitely in one of these. Of course by nursing them so much some anglers end up playing 'mother' to the worms and never get round to chopping them up for groundbait or sticking them on the hook. Never get too attached to your wormery is my motto.

An easy way to make a wormery is by using plastic sacks or heavy-duty bin liners. The compost of leaves, newsprint, grass cuttings etc., plus the worms are tipped into the sacks, which have the necks left open for easy air circulation. Provided they are kept cool in somewhere like a garage, they will not only last months, but can breed as well. If you stand the plastic sacks outside they will fare even better, provided you top up with peelings and fruit. But protect against the frost at all costs. Wormeries can be constructed anywhere but naturally they must be enclosed so you can get the worms out when required.

For hooking the lobworm, if it's big you will either want a big hook, or you can simply use the flattened tail section for the hookbait, and put the rest in the groundbait. If the lobworm is of average size and you want the bigger fish, then try hooking it through the 'collar', which is the strongest part of the body and does not contain anything vital. There is also a book on the market called *Small-Scale Earthworm Breeding* which may assist you if you are a serious worm angler. I like to hook my worms about three times through the centre section of the body, to allow for the tugs and pulls of unwanted small fish.

Perch and eels are the bane of the worm angler, but I can't help you with that!

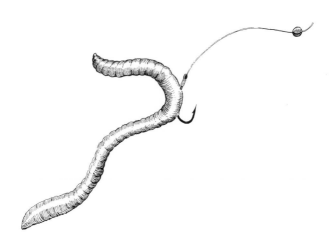

Above: Sarah Bennet cast out a minute later with the same bait and landed this Throop barbel.

Right: Jerry Airey took this barbel on a piece of barbecue sausage in bean juice.

Below: There is a beauty in the colour of this tiny minnow's spawning garb. When legered on the bottom it will attract chub and big perch.

A modern tackle shop will offer a wide variety of 'stimulator' groundbait additives. Match anglers use them on their own while pleasure anglers mix them with white or brown groundbait and hold the fish in the swim longer.

Mixed up properly with a good flavouring, this Z72 groundbait makes both a loose feed and a hookbait. When fish feed on groundbait and ignore the hookbaits, that is the time to mould some groundbait into a paste for a hookbait.

Coloured multi-purpose groundbaits are important to match anglers—the flavour and colour enhances catch rates.

Facing page: The placing of the groundbait and the texture of the mix is all-important when fishing in a fast-flowing river like the Hampshire Avon. If you have barbel or chub in mind, mix some of your loose feed into the groundbait mix and wedge in a stone. This will keep it on the bottom.

Wasp grubs make a deadly bait for chub in slow to medium pace rivers—especially when fished under the float. Feed with maggots and put a wasp grub on the hook to isolate it amongst the loose feed.

To obtain wasp cake, contact your local council who remove them from houses.

This is a cross section of a wasp nest or 'cake'. When the grubs take up nearly all the cavity they are ready to use.

The chub love a tasty wasp grub and will take them almost as fast as you can throw them in.

Prawns and shrimps work well as baits in weir pools or gravel runs below rapids, while extracts mixed into paste baits can be fished in stillwaters.

Slugs are more successful when legered or
freelined in a river rather than a lake.

Crayfish

Crayfish is a difficult bait to obtain in these times of increased industrial and farmland pollution, since it likes clean, clear water. Crayfish can attain a length of some four inches in British waters although one and a half to two inches is the size the angler should look for. They can be found under stones and boulders in rivers and streams that run through chalk, limestone and sandstone, and they look like miniature black lobsters. To keep them you need a sizeable plastic bait bucket and an aerator. They are a good indication of how clean a river is, being among the first freshwater crustaceans to disappear when pollution levels become intolerable.

As well as on the river bed, they can be found under the camp sheathing which is sometimes prolific in chalkstream areas, though sunken branches are always worth looking under too. They swim backwards, flipping that fan-like tail in short, hard jerks. As soon as you lift a stone or boulder to grab one you will appreciate its turn of speed.

They are primarily a chub bait, but barbel will take them as well. Hook just once half way down the tail and cast out gently. You will fish them best on a running leger, where you ignore the trembling as it chugs around the bottom, and wait for the rod top to fold over. A big chub, even with its cavernous mouth, still needs a bit of time, maybe a second or two, to get a crayfish well inside its mouth.

Crayfish is a good bait, but it is becoming increasingly difficult to find due to the effluent from the many trout fisheries now in operation on rivers like the Hampshire Avon. There, where the bottom used to be covered with clean gravel (an ideal habitat for crayfish), a brown algea scum now covers the stones. Doubtless the investigation into trout farm effluent will show them to be a contributory factor in the decline of water life in many rivers.

Facing page: An angler waits for a bite as sunset descends on beautiful Lough Garadice in Co Leitrim in Ireland.

Groundbaits

With the exception of perhaps the predators, any freshwater species the angler is likely to pursue will respond to groundbaiting. That is, throwing into the swim a mixture of crumb, bread, bran or whatever you can lay your hands on that is remotely edible in an effort to draw fish into the swim. Attracting a particular species into the area you are fishing is important, but remember you want to give them a 'teaser', not something which they are going to stuff themselves to the gills on and then miss your hookbaits. In quiet canals you may only need a bait tin full of white cloudbait to attract the small fry in, whereas in Ireland, where vast shoals of bream roam the waters like locusts in a cornfield, you probably couldn't throw in enough to hold them in front of you. The size of the water, the number of fish it holds and the species you are pursuing must all be taken into consideration, and only experience, failures and success will tell you the amount and type of groundbait to use.

In strong rivers you are going to need something stiff and heavy that will sink down quickly and not break up until it hits the bottom. In a quiet backwater of that very same river, a mixture of cloudbait and light crumb would be more appropriate. As many as two hundred years ago fishermen appreciated the need to attract fish by groundbaiting, and I suspect that the earliest human life in the Polynesian islands used groundbait in the sea to attract fish close to where they could be trapped or speared.

The freshwater angler must learn to distinguish between groundbaiting, which is the throwing in of bait on the same day as you fish, and pre-baiting which is throwing in quantities of bait several days before you wish to fish. Pre-baiting is a lot easier so far as judging quantities goes, for if you put down too much and you put the fish off with that initial bombardment, it's not too vital as you won't be fishing straight away, and the fish can settle in on it during the night.

Groundbaiting on the other hand requires a lot less in the way of quantity, but needs to be introduced into the water with a little more finesse. The easiest all-round groundbait is made from bread and bran. I use this mostly as a prebaiting mixture as it can be quite filling and the fish need a couple of days to get through it. If you are using breadflake as a hookbait it would seem natural to use stale loaves as the groundbait. To do this you need to soak a few old loaves in a bucket of water, mush them up into a pulp and then strain off the surplus water. This groundbait is good for tench and bream.

Alternatively, you could cut the loaves into slices, bake them hard in the oven, then crumble them down into a powder and mix up the powder with water at the bankside. It makes for a slower sinking groundbait that can be used in small quantities while you are actually fishing.

The same mushed up bread can be padded out by adding some bran, but this swells the mixture and it won't squeeze into balls hard enough for throwing long distances.

For making a good cloudbait of a white texture simply bake the slices of white bread very hard in the oven, taking care not to burn them, then grind them into a very fine powder. This will give you a fine white cloudbait. To obtain a brown cloudbait, simply follow the same instructions but use only the crusts of the loaves.

It's now easy to walk into your local tackle shop and buy either a 56-lb sack or a 2-lb pack of ready-made commercial groundbait.

As an important part of the angler's bait armoury there are dozens of specialised groundbaits on the market for use on different species, and under different fishing conditions. The top French matchmen for instance concentrate on mixing a groundbait of sufficient properties to get the bloodworm and jokers down in the water in a column, and not spreading them out over a large area. Feeding the tiny jokers is considered bad form as you could then pull fish up from the bottom and spread them out. Some of the favourite French groundbait ingredients are bread, maize, hempseed, soil and peanuts. I have mentioned in the bloodworm section that worms can be kept in a peat mixture riddled into newspaper. While there is obviously a lot in the way of additives, scents and flavours that the matchmen could mix in, to them it is much more important to get those precious bloodworms and jokers down to the bottom. Cornmeal, otherwise known as ground maize, is good for bream and adds a slight yellow tinge to any mix. Peanuts, in powder form are used mainly with the soil as a binder, but the nut does produce an oily slick which helps attract the fish.

Some of the vast selection of perhaps somewhat strange additives in powder or grain form as used by the pro matchmen on the continent are as follows. Pigeon droppings (think of the eel and catfish anglers!) are a good roach attractor, and the best droppings are reputed to come from the pigeons that are fed on hempseed (presumably the oil content of the hempseed is passed through the bird). Chalk powder is used to hold feed together and to give it white colouring, while coconut husk is used in its fine ground form as an additive for both surface and bottom feeds. Egg powder is used as a surface mix when fishing for rudd or bream and sunflower seeds in their powdered form are also used as surface additives. Considered as a stimulant to start the bottom fish feeding, is the herb, fennel. Mollasses is also used for bottom feed. Obviously very sticky and sweet, it is ideal for bream though not so good for the angler who finds it messy.

Finally, there is aloe. The only aloe I knew of was aloe butter which is a product derived from a plant that is used to soothe sunburn, and I know about that from my many marlin trips to tropical waters. But the continental match anglers use aloe for its strong laxative powers, allowing the fish to pass the feed straight through and stay hungry. I cannot confirm this personally . . . and no, I'm not about to take some!

That's a very rough sample of match groundbaits and additives for you to experiment with, and mix up in your own quantities. In the tackle shop you can buy all the premixed groundbaits you want, whether for match or pleasure fishing. The most popular with the pleasure angler is the white crumb.

Ground down commercially by firms like British Groundbaits, you can buy it either by the kilo in small packs or in 25 kilo sacks. Used on its own it mixes into a fairly firm, fast-breaking groundbait but by adding more powder to dry it out, the texture can be stiffened to concrete where it will crash to the bottom and presumably stay until it breaks down a few days later. It is best mixed with some brown crumb which is a looser mix and will help it break up easier, usually on impact with the water. In fast, deep rivers you will need to add a binding agent like golden breadcrumb to get it down near the bottom. Even then you may have to put in a stone to aid sinking.

The white and brown groundbaits come in about five types: brown fine, brown coarse, white fine, white coarse, and pink fine. The latter is used as a slow sink feed for roach and rudd. From here you can take a step over to the prebagged groundbait counter and spend as much time (and money) as you wish in procuring as many and varied groundbaits in colours and additives as you want. A few of the more popular ones have been used to good effect in matches and for pleasure fishermen seeking good bags of quality fish.

The biggest selection, indeed possibly the best selection come from the European leaders in the field called Sensas. Over five years the Sensas company has sponsored the French national pole fishing team. They offer a range of 40 baits and 200 types of flour, with instructions translated into four languages printed on the bags. Some of the better surface feeds are as follows.

Roubaisien is a light and aromatic feed for all canals and lakes, ideal for roach, bream and dace. Gradually moisten to produce a supple, non sticky paste. If required, add fine grain sand. Use a small portion for each cast. For bottom fishing add soil and make bigger, tighter balls.

Michiels Ablette is a surface cloudbait for dace and bleak. Mix in with only the finest crumb, and use with pinkies and bread punch for best results, feeding little and often.

Explosif is an explosive cloud mix for still waters and canals that can be added to Roubaisien for increased bites.

Record 515 is one of the top surface feeds. It produces a dense yellow cloud and is good for bream. To prepare a fragrant mist in the water, moisten flour to almost a liquid state and allow to dry slightly. Fish on the little and often basis.

Michiels Canal is blended groundbait for all types of canal fishing where the requirement is for the feed to break slowly and seductively from the surface.

Z72. My first insight into the success of this groundbait was when I was on a magazine assignment down at lakes near Ringwood. The local matchmen had bagged up on some tench and their hands were dyed red. They were using Z72 red with the flavouring from the bottle added as both an additive to the brown fine groundbait, and as a mix for a paste as well—for hookbaits I hasten to add! A general all round groundbait, mixed as follows. In a clean bait container moisten contents thoroughly, and add some of the special mixture supplied in the pack. The creation when thrown in should create a haze radiating in all directions, and consistency can be regulated by adding more water.

Magic (in the natural or yellow). A superb bottom feed for roach, bream, tench or chub. Gradually moisten to obtain a sticky paste. Form solid balls of the mix and place these on the bottom about ten minutes before fishing. It is very successful when mixed slightly overwet, allowed to dry or having a little extra dry powder added (to the mix), then kneaded into a paste for hookbaits. Fished over the top of the feed it can be excellent. It can also be used as an additive to a heavy mix like coarse white or brown crumb, with the addition of crushed hemp and spices.

Coco Belge, or coconut flour is the ground husk, not the actual white coconut and is excellent when mixed with coarse brown bread for bream.

Tilt is for pole anglers, to add to the pigeon droppings and resultant hempseed oil they are fed on. Barbel have been known to take a hookbait of this made into a paste with the addition of some golden breadcrumb. Primarily it is a surface feed. For still or stagnant waters gradually moisten the mix to obtain a smooth, non-sticky paste. Toss in only small, lightly rolled balls, as the feed is strong, and you want to induce the fish to feed slowly. For flowing waters you can enrich the bait with the additon of fine grained clay dust to increase weight and sinking speeds. Form large, tightly rolled balls and throw in sufficiently far upstream from the area selected for fishing. If the luring effect of the bait diminishes, repeat a scattering of small, tightly rolled balls within range of the fishing area. Ground hemp is always successful when used on rivers and fished in conjunction with the swimfeeder and caster as hookbait.

For bigger fish, Sensas provide Rich-Pro, a high-protein paste bait for large carp and tench that does not need to be introduced; en masse to a new water just a few balls thrown in around the hookbait will be enough. Another is Big Sensas—the ultimate big fish stillwater groundbait with high-protein additives that attracts bream, tench and carp, or Michiels Special Food, a meaty bottom groundbait for all types of water, that specialises in attracting bream, tench, roach, barbel and chub.

On the British groundbaits scene you have a good surface cloudbait in Cosmic Cloud, which for maximum cloud effect you must mix wet and sloppy, using roughly a measure of water to a measure of groundbait. For surface fishing use wet, sloppy walnut-size balls, and for bottom feeding or mid-water use firm golf-ball sizes. It should produce a milky cloud that just hangs in the water, and dissolves its fruity-sweet flavours and soluble attractors. There are some silver particles which flash as the cloud sinks, hopefully attracting other small fish into the area. Ideal for roach, rudd, bleak, small carp and bream.

Katch is a hemp and herb attractor blended according to a secret French recipe, and mixed to enable easy presentation of ground hemp and other attractant additives. When mixed it should sink slowly to the bottom, releasing particles, bubbles and natural flavours which work in the swim to attract all species. Katch is good for chub and barbel when fished in a fast-flowing river, where the additives pull fish from downstream. For maximum bubbling and particle action, make it into a fairly dry mix. Add a quarter to a third measure of water to one measure of Katch. Squeeze golf-ball-sized balls softly for slow sinking. For surface feeding make into a wet mix, and use small walnut-sized balls.

Meatiemix is a special blend of dried red meat, rusk and essential additives that provides a balanced protein groundbait. It can also be made into a stiff paste for hookbait and is particularly successful for chub, carp, tench and barbel. Put some water in your groundbait bowl then add the groundbait, fluffing and aerating the mix and allowing it to expand and absorb water slowly. For bottom fishing and deep waters use anything up to compact tennis ball sizes. For surface feeding and use as a cloudbait, mix wet and sloppy, throwing in walnut-sized pieces.

Freshwater Fishing Baits

Contest contains a unique blend of German spice flavours and soluble sweet attractors, all researched as being the best for bream fishing. For mixing, pour water into your groundbait bowl, add the powder and allow it to absorb and expand as you mix. It might pay you to leave it a few minutes to dry then gradually add a little more water until the desired texture is achieved. The mixture can be enhanced with the addition of vanilla flavouring, especially if you have a shoal of bream in mind. Many of these pre-packs are intended for use in match fishing, but by adding them into your ordinary groundbaits like brown or white crumb they definitely enhance the mix, and I am certain keep the fish in the swim for longer.

I remember only recently on Lough Garadice in Ireland on the Connolly shore, we were staying with top local expert Dennis Breen and he had just introduced nearly 100 lb of white crumb and crushed maize into two swims in an effort to induce the bream to come in. The shoals on this Irish water are horrendous, and have had echo soundings taken of them over half a mile long, so we were really just scratching the surface. We arrived at dawn to find bream rolling over a quarter mile square, in fact I thought they must be ill from the amount of groundbait we had dumped in. One of my friends Jerry Airey mixed up and threw in some yellow groundbait, but flavoured and coloured; it was only a few pounds and it seemed a piffling amount after the previous night's barrage. Imagine my surprise when one of the bream I later landed was spewing yellow groundbait everywhere. I had laughed . . . but it damn well worked!

Baits of Yesteryear

If you think some of the modern-day boilie baits are unusual, you may be surprised to learn of unusual concoctions used by anglers in the past. Fishermen have always been searching for that 'magic' bait that will bring fish to the net on every cast. Such a bait doesn't exist of course, because any species of fish being hammered for any length of time on a particular bait will develop its fear senses to avoid that bait in the future. Then you have to start all over again and look for something new! One such weird and wonderful bait of the past was boiled wheat. First soaked in cold water to cleanse it, it was placed in a thermos flask of boiling water to cook itself. However I once heard from an old boy who still uses it that one day he filled the flask to full and it exploded on him as the wheat expanded! Exploding flasks are hazardous things on a riverbank!

Those curious little creatures the woodlice were also popular in the past. Found under logs, stones and brickwork, and kept in a tin of moss they were very popular for big roach in their heyday. Of course many an angler's house has since collapsed as he searched through his brickwork for more woodlice.

Wasp grubs were once particularly good for chub. The poor old grubs were tender and soft skinned anyway, but the anglers of the time then steamed, baked or boiled them, one presumes to soften them still further. One also assumes that mamma wasp wasn't around to see what these anglers were doing to their progeny.

What do you do with weed? Like me you probably haul it out with a double-backed weed drag and throw it up the bank. Not so our fastidious fishermen from the pre-war era. They scrabbled about on weir sills draping their hooks with silkweed and then catching netfuls of dace. This practice generally came to an abrupt halt when the lock keeper came down and started unscrewing the valves on the weir. It's amazing how little traction you get from wet wellies on weed when you want to move fast!

Pearl Barley. No, not the singer, the bait man, the bait. These little grains were stewed until they became soft and then used by dace anglers who subsequently caught roach. Such anglers could be heard on moonlit nights as they boiled up their bait, singing, 'Won't you come home Pearl Bailey? Won't you come home?'

Freshwater Fishing Baits

Grasshoppers were once mounted on a large hook and dangled near overhanging bushes for large chub—sorry 'chevin'—that lurked beneath with their big salivering mouths. But old Gerty grasshopper took one look at those chub and hopped back up in the bushes. Chub anglers could always be recognised as they thrashed through the bushes trying to recover both jumping grasshopper and tangled line. They were responsible for many of the early bank clearing expeditions.

Talking of things that jump, how about frogs? I joke not, young Freddy frog was a prime bait for pike, chub and perch. Simple to use, but a sonofabitch to catch. To rig you simply 'kill the frog by a flip on the head with the finger before placing it on the hook. Put the hook in at its tail and out the mouth, a shot being pinched on the cast a short distance above the hook and the hind legs tied with fine silk just above the shot.' Simple isn't it? If I had to do that the RSPCF (Royal Society for the Prevention of Cruelty to Frogs) would arrest me, and the police charge me with being a transvestite due to the large amounts of silk on my person.

Which reminds me of an episode I once had in Ireland when I was fishing Lough Garadice in Co. Leitrim. Nigel Newport and I were on a dawn session for pike on the Connolly shore. We had a pair of deadbaits each and were working our way along the bank, when an old boy appeared out of a hedge near my shoulder, making me start.

'G'mornin to you!'

'Morning!' we replied.

He shuffled closer until he was a full three inches from my ear, wafts of the previous night's Guinness and whiskey chaser invading my nostrils. If I'd struck a match the two of us would have exploded into a ball of flames.

'Tell me now lads, would ye have seen anything of me frog loin?'

I looked at Nigel who stared back at me blank faced.

'Your what?'

'Are t'be soir. O'i can't find me frog line anywhere."

I wondered just how must Guinness he had drunk. I tried to be polite. 'You did say frog line didn't you?' The question was answered by a question.

Baits of Yesteryear

'Are yooz lads poick fishin' then? Cos if ye are ye had better watch out for moby. I almost had him in the other night. It was he who took me frog loin.'

It now transpired that this gentleman might possibly be an obscure member of the Irish Pike Anglers Club, and had indeed perfected a method of application that resulted in the landing of very big pike.

'Ye see lads to catch the poick in here ye have to bait up wi a big ole froggie on a string, cast him out as far ye might, and tie the other end te a strong place like a boulder or tree. I usually check me frog loin every four days, but I can't find it.'

His eyes narrowed as the story reached its height, and he said in a whisper, 'Oi reckon ole moby has been away with him.'

He winked and nodded, like he had a knowing sort of perpetual twitch. I smiled and looked at Nigel who was red with trying to restrain a laugh. He looked at our tackle, gently touched the rods so they made the optonics beep-beep and with a look of horror at rods that 'beeped', scurried away. We both folded up with laughter.

Then Nigel said, 'You know what method we're using here don't you? By changing positions along the bank trying to find the pike?'

I shrugged my shoulders.

'We're bloody LEAPFROGGING aren't we!'

The still Irish air rocked with our laughter and I missed seeing a cow tread on my rod holder. As I chased it away, it calmly halted, looked at me with large brown innocent eyes, lifted its tail and dropped a gallon of the best right onto my landing net mesh! Pooooh! The moral of this little story is to never extract the Michael too much.

The following morning we worked our pike rods the opposite way along Connolly shore. I saw Nigel stoop into the water and slowly pull in hand over hand, a length of twine. One end led up the bank and was tied to the top of a bundle of boulders, that had fallen in a crumpled heap. As I walked up he pulled the last of the twine out of the water, and we looked in awe at the severed end. Yes, it had to be the old man's frog loin . . . and moby had claimed another victim!

Another dace bait for the autumn float angler was procured in a strange way. The angler simply hung up a folded hessian sack in the garden for a couple of days, then the day he went fishing he opened the sack to find it full of . . . earwigs. No, it's true. Earwigs were all the rage in the thirties and forties, so don't stamp on 'em anymore, they may be worth £3 a pint in the tackle shops.

The Thames tideway dace used to have a particular fancy for red flannel. Apparently you baited your hooks with small strips of red flannel, although of course if the dace were well and truly 'on' you could end up cutting into strips both legs of your trousers.

Pieces of bacon fat were excellent for barbel, dace and roach, with particular attention being paid to the inner rind of stringy bacon. Now this isn't as stupid as it sounds, because in the early sixties I watched an angler take a piece of bacon fat out of his sandwich, put it on the hook and catch an $11^1/4$-lb barbel from the car park pool on the lower Royalty. As Max Boyce says, 'I know, cos I was there!' I also remember those awful breakfasts at local establishments and can well see how the barbel had an affinity for two sausages, bacon, fried slice bread and tomatoes floating in a pool of fat.

Greaves, a waxy thing, was popular for barbel and chub. It was soaked cold, or boiled for half an hour before using.

What a lot of pith and brains I hear you say. Yet these two items were a responsible bait for the winter chub enthusiast to use. Pith, often used by an angler with a lisp wishing to relieve himself, was really the spinal marrow from a bullock. The outer skin was removed (from the marrow, not the whole bullock you fools) and the pith washed in changes of water. Cut into pieces the size of hazelnuts it was used as the hookbait. Brains, on the other hand were tied up in a cloth and boiled for an hour until hard. Minced up they were then used as a groundbait and thrown in the swim with a ladle. This can get quite expensive of course depending how many ladles you throw in. The brains by the way come from the bullock, who one assumes is in an advanced state of death, having had his bone marrow extracted by the angler first.

One of the age old sayings came from the first angler to crack the 50 lb of chub barrier using this bait, as fellow club members watched him in awe . . . 'I don't believe it Sam, he must be taking the pith!' As for previous generations taking fish on unusual baits, we don't do too badly ourselves.

Baits of Yesteryear

As I write this, just three days ago I was fishing for barbel and Chub on Throop fishery on the Dorset Stour. It was hot. My brains were cooked, Jerry had a pith, and we loose fed my red flannels and earwigs. Bored with the continual crash bites from grasshoppers and frogs, Jerry's girlfriend Sarah decided it was time to put the gas on and cook dinner. Seemed like a reasonable suggestion, except that she screwed the apparatus together wrongly and a full canister of gas escaped into the air. No hot tea, no bangers, beans, fried eggs or custard! Disaster. The tins had also already been opened. Well, Jerry is not one to waste an opportunity and went for a two-hour sulk along the bank. I could see barbel in the swim, but in the bright sunlight and 80 degree temperature they were having nothing. I bait dropped everything I could lay my hands on into the swim: luncheon meat, cheese, sweetcorn. The barbel looked more active, then Jerry came back. He picked up a dripping barbecue banger and beans tin, took out a sausage, broke off a chunk and baiting, cast out. Three seconds later he hooked a barbel of about 4 lb. As we weighed and photographed it Sarah cast out a banger in sauce and hooked a 6 pounder! No honestly, that's the truth. Would I lie to you?

Other anglers have caught on even more weird and wonderful baits, and many are still not an arrestable offence. If you think that the anglers of yesteryear had crazy bait ideas I can assure you that some of our top specimen hunters use baits that would fit in either a cookery book, a laboratory or a zoo! I telephoned top eel specialist John Sidley for an insight into some of the unusual eel baits that he uses to extract not just specimen eels but hordes of the wrigglers, enough to give the wife a nightmare.

'What do you mean unusual baits?' asked John, with that dry Birmingham accent. 'These aren't my unusual baits . . . I use them all the time and catch good eels too.' It transpired from our conversation that if an eel water is notoriously hard then John has to get the eels into a feeding mood, and he does this by throwing in . . . wait for it . . . chicken guts! Yyuuurrrgh! Apparently if he pre-baits the water with anything that has a fish-based smell to it, he gets only pike moving in, and he has never had an eel under those conditions.

'Big eels are loners' he told me, 'they won't come in if a pike or a

Freshwater Fishing Baits

shoal of perch are over the baits.' His bait of the moment is liver closely followed by roes of fish, mussels, sections of dead frog, other eels, whole or half dead toads, and the *piece de resistance?* Dead baby birds. Yes, they have a lot of air resistance when cast!

John was put on to the idea of using meat-based groundbaits by an old boy who used to gut his chickens at the lakeside. 'Fish there' he told John, 'and you'll catch a big eel.' So he fished there. And he caught a big eel. After that chicken guts were a regular on the eel waters around his home.

'I look for anything dead in the road' he told me. 'Mice, birds, and the like, but a squashed hedgehog is a real delicacy. I've tried ox blood but it attracts only tench and bream. As I said before, the eels are loners and won't come in the swim if other shoal fish are there.'

As an enthusiast of oils I asked John if he had tried any of the sea fishing oil concentrates.

'Oh yes, I use them in a swimfeeder, soaking the oil in a . . .'

He stopped in mid sentence.

'What do you soak them in John?' I was curious now. 'A piece of cloth?'

'No.'

'Well some cotton wool then?'

'No, but you're getting warmer, very much warmer in fact.'

I couldn't think what on earth it was.

'It's about the most absorbent material you can think of' he said. 'You can get them in chemist shops.' I knew what he used. Jumping catfish I must try that myself.

And talking of jumping catfish my next call got me through to Vic Gillings, one of the country's leading experts in catfishing. It was no surprise to learn from him that 'exotics' produced fish for him though I confess to never hearing of bream being caught on fillets of mackerel. Vic has had loads of them though, but his favourite bait for both big catfish and carp is a nice juicy lamb's kidney . . . minus the lamb of course! He assured me that such delicacies as prawns, liver and rabbit guts were held in high esteem by anglers in pursuit of the 'big pussy', or catfish as the more eloquent know them. He has heard of other specialist catfish anglers having a preference for skinned

110

mice, but thinks it doesn't really matter what bait you have at a catfish venue like Claydon, where the baits are never more than 30 feet from a cat. At the moment he is experimenting with something called pheronomes, one of the products said to 'send fish crackers . . . or your money back!' Like my own experiments with such liquid lovelies, Vic has yet to find any appreciable difference in the catch rate, although fish certainly do take them.

So there you have an insight into weird baits past and present. Whether you are a bit short on the pith and brains, have got your greaves caught in a mangle, or can't find a lamb to donate its kidneys, you can be assured that almost anything, if edible will be consumed with degrees of avidity by Mr Fish.

Which brings me to the ultimate cult in ultra baits that you can't get in the tackle shop. Many anglers will know I specialise in fishing for 'Big' fish. I'm not fussy—as long as it's over 100 lb I'm satisfied. So how about a bait for one of my favourite species, the Tiger shark? In its stomach have been found the following, and I can only put it down to some pretty crazy angler on a pre-baiting schedule: fish, crab, turtles (with shell), stingrays, birds, other sharks, porpoises, dogs, rats, a crocodile's head, a wooden tom-tom, clothing, boat cushions, driftwood, lumps of coal, a two-pound coil of copper wire, assorted nuts and bolts, the hind leg of a sheep, human flesh and limbs plus a car number plate, and a five-gallon drum.

And the weirdest bait I've ever caught a fish on myself? Twelve miles into the Gulfstream off the coast of Florida, the skipper of the *Ace* gameboat, Captain Jim Taylor, rigged me up with a whole dead squirrel he found in the road, wired onto two 10/0 mustad hooks. Deep jigging in several hundred feet of water I took a 60-lb Amberjack . . . and it didn't even crease the fur!

This then, is a basic guide to either introduce you to, or refresh old memories of the baits that have caught fish. There are those among you who feel the more complicated the bait, the better your chance of success. My friends I tell you, it is very often of little consequence what bait you use, but how, where, and when you use it. Any of the baits mentioned will catch fish at some time or other. It is up to you, as a fisherman, to find out just which one works on the day.

	Bread	Worms	Cheese	Sweetcorn	Fish	Boilies	Floaters	Pastes	Nuts	Maggots	Wasp Grub	Caster	Seeds	Blood-worm
Carp	X	X	X	X		X	X	X	X	X		X	X	
Chub	X	X	X	X	X	X	X	X		X	X	X		
Barbel	X	X	X	X		X		X		X	X	X		
Dace	X	X	X	X						X		X		X
Pike		X			X									
Perch		X		X	X					X	X	X		X
Eels		X	X		X			X		X				
Tench	X	X	X	X		X		X	X	X		X	X	X
Zander		X			X									
Catfish		X	X		X	X		X		X				
Roach	X	X	X	X				X		X	X	X	X	X
Rudd	X	X	X	X			X			X		X	X	X
Bream	X	X		X		X		X		X		X		X

Table for popularity of each bait to different species